YOUR VIBRATION IS THE KEY

"Unlock Your True Potential and Happiness"

Parth P. Vyas PH.D.

Nexus Stories Publication
Bhārata

YOUR VIBRATION IS THE KEY

(Written by Parth P. Vyas PH.D.)

2021

ISBN # 978-93-91529-06-2

Publication

Nexus Stories Publication, Surat (Gujarat), Bhārata

https://nexus-stories.com

+91 87800 80718

NEXUS STORIES PUBLICATION

Surat, Gujarat, India.

First Published by Nexus Stories 2021
Copyright © Parth P. Vyas 2021
All Rights Reserved.

ISBN # 978-93-91529-06-2

This book is dedicated:

To my god, the creator and the Supreme Energy. It was under divine guidance that the information regarding vibration contained in this book was received.

To my parents, who taught me to believe in myself and have strong faith on me. My mother always told me that God always hears and answers our prayers

To my wife, who compiled the writing for this book, and who assisted me during my journey. She is appreciated so much more than I could ever express.

To my son, who inspire me, who is my friend and close to my heart.

To all my spiritual Leaders and teachers, who taught me the true essence of life in my spiritual journey and always inspire me.

To my friends, doctors and Spiritual healers, who help me and put their efforts to make this book possible.

And to those I have yet to meet, may your paths lead you to the place of greatest peace and abundant goodness.

Table of Contents

INTRODUCTION

Do you vibrate with love, abundance, joy, fear, wrath, wealth, failure, or peace?

The vibrations that you put into the world gives you back what you believe in and experience. If you believe in love, then love is returned to you. You get hate back if you believe in hate.

Then how do you understand whatever vibrations you bring into the universe? Look at what you get in your life to learn what you bring into the world. Most of your vibrations are below your conscious level. They are life's values, people and yourself. In your life, you actively strive to affirm your convictions as valid. So, if you believe people rip off when you find someone to be told and you see yourself how that's, it is. Then your confidence and energy are strengthened, and you will continue to draw more, and the cycle continues.

One way to crack this circle is to use strategies like NLP (Neuro Linguistic Program), Rapid Eye, EFT, Different Healing Modalities and Hypnosis for energy clearing. Using these methods, you will determine when ideologies began to release the convictions and emotions that no longer serve you. Use your aware and unconscious mind to change your convictions and emotions. You can change your values and emotions and change what you draw into your life.

Emotional Freedom Technique (EFT) and Rapid Eye Technology (RET), along with many other techniques, have been created to make it possible to release the energy of deep-seated values and emotions that adversely affect our lives.

In the Emotional Freedom Technique and Rapid Eye Technology, we can take the centre of the convictions and feelings to a deep, energy-intensive level. Most of us don't believe our emotions are an option. But the fact is that our emotions are the product of our assumption that we are conscious and unconscious at the same time. This is so many people will live and have different feelings about the same experience. Your confidence in an event, word or experience defines your feeling.

If you can change your views about life and yourself, your feelings can change. When your emotions change, your vibration changes. You stop the negative circle and start another more positive circle that brings you what you want and deserve in your life.

******

"Everything is energy. Match the frequency of the reality you want and you cannot help but get that reality. It can be no other way. This is not philosophy. This is physics."

— Albert Einstein

CHAPTER ONE

<u>Introducing Vibration</u>

You probably heard this expression, "raise your vibration," or maybe "I get good vibrations."

It might be difficult to believe, but everything on and beyond this world is vibration. Things seem solid to our eyes, but what we don't see is that the whole universe is made of vibrant, solid particles.

But to understand what many spiritual teachers speak about when they speak of vibration, you need to have a simple understanding of the truth of the quantum universe around you – the world that's so thin, you can't even see it on a microscope.

Vibration awareness will awaken many things in you.

It will be easier for you to realize how we are all linked and why compassion and kindness are so necessary.

The Vibration Science

Everything around you consist of vibrating particles and electricity.

The vibration speed makes things look solid, liquid or gas.

This idea is difficult to grasp since, right now, you don't fall through the floor.

You clearly keep a telephone or look at the computer screen and cannot just run your hand like air.

On the quantum level, however, super-minute particles bounce off each other as you try to run your hand over your computer screen or phone.

The particles that vibrate against each other create resistance and prevent one another from moving through.

Think of a powerful magnet.

It's hard to bring two magnets together.

There seems to be an invisible force field, which prevents them from touching, no matter how difficult you try.

This invisible force field is made of small particles, which are opposed to one another and refuse to collide. Of course, this is a straightforward description, but you should research chemistry and quantum physics to grasp all the things at stake.

Positive vibes and negative vibes

These waves are completely unseen to us because they are too tiny to look at.

When we look at a solid entity, we see the effect that several parts vibrate together (so many, there isn't quite a number that you can understand). Much of what you see consists of empty space. Read all about an atom structure if you're interested!

Think of a minute's vibration.

What kind of feelings arise if you think about something that vibrates very slowly?

What about fast?

You are possibly very energetic and exciting with high vibration and slowness and sadness with low vibration.

If we speak of "increasing the vibration," we speak of a simply higher-speed vibration.

Hope, love, kindness and compassion are all very easily vibrating feelings.

At lower speeds, greed, terror, hatred and sadness vibrate.

High and low vibration evidence

Sand that is exposed to various frequencies, a method called cymatics, is the best way to see the results of vibrations. Cymatics allow us to imagine the effect of various vibrations.

You will note that the lower vibrations produce broad, slightly boring forms. Some people find these types of disagreeable.

As the vibrations increase, the forms become complex, detailed and beautiful. Higher vibrations and frequencies create more friendly 'feel good' effects.

Dr Masaru Emoto carried out an experiment to look at the results of our words' vibrations.

Simply saying one word to another, without feeling or emotion, he was able to observe that positive words produced crystals of a greater vibration similar to high sand vibration in cymatics experiments.

Negative words have created crystals that looked like lower energy vibrations.

Elevate the vibration

Positiveness, empathy, kindness, hope, as you can see, have higher vibrations than negative, fear and hate. When you look at the cymatics experiments and the water crystals of Dr Emoto, it is easy to understand why you want to increase the vibration.

There are many ways the vibration can be increased.

You should try all kinds of meditations, workouts, spiritual activities and energize.

In the end, your vibration will be raised by your emphasis on love and compassion. Some routes will make it quicker and easier for you.

Everyone is different, so try some various approaches and see how you feel. You will know that your pulse increases because you feel more confident, relaxed, satisfied and kind.

Does yoga make you feel like that?

Map Your Vibration

Do you ever have one of the maps with the "you are here" sticker, which shows how you vibrate? Are you going the right way? Are you closer to your targets or even in the right direction?

Abraham-Hicks speaks of an individual driving from city to city. You do not have a map, and you do not understand that you are very close to your destination, so you turn around and go back to the starting point. We all might be tempted to do so if we feel like our vibration has changed, but nothing seems to change. If we do not know how close we are to where we want to be, it can be frustrating. That's where we want our vibration to be mapped.

As in geography, various types of maps provide various types of information. We must use various maps to determine our vibration.

3 Map of the vibration steps:

1. Your current life maps

The situation in your current life maps your previous vibration. Your past vibration has brought you to where you are now. If you like it, then you want to concentrate on more and better stuff. If you do not, do NOT work to change the vibration by focussing on where you want to go.

2. Evidence Map:

All signs of proof that the stuff you want show you what you're currently vibrating. These are also called driftwood. If anyone else around you has what you want, you see what you want on TV, something that comes close to what you want, or you almost get what you want. These are positive signs that she's on her way, so celebrate. Hint: the more you notice driftwood, the more you experience.

3. Feelings Map:

How much of the time do you feel? This will tell you what is happening next. ALL you put on a fake smiley face and pretend that you are happy if you do not. If we're frank, we know how happy we are most of the time. Here's the thing, don't beat yourself over it if you're not content. That would totally defeat the goal because it would not make you happier! Just try to feel better every day a little bit. Work up the scale your way. Even if you're upset or angry when you're down, reach a neutral position is a major improvement that will make improvements.

It's good not to resist your emotions and to tell stories that make you feel worse. Just let yourself feel and be there for yourself. Self-love is one of the easiest ways to boost your vibration.

Where do you feel right now like you are? Remember that you decide how and what ideas you want to concentrate on. I would like to hear all your thoughts about how you stay focused if you don't know exactly how close you are to the next thing you dream about.

Frustrated by the attraction law?

How can people work for them?

Learn how to do this. Get the flow of your magic and build a life that you enjoy. Even if you don't want to deal with the rule of attraction, practising personal alchemy increases your harmony, love and happiness in life. Personal alchemy provides you with the rest of the process required to make your life easy and enjoyable. It's just the missing ingredient you expected.

__What Is Vibrational Energy?__

You are a living field of energy. Your body is made up of particles producing energy, each in continuous motion. You are vibrating and generating light, just like anything and everyone else in the world.

The field of vibrational medicine, also called vibrational energy, is used to optimize your wellbeing by and around your body

The idea of energy fields in the body can sound more spiritual than therapeutic for many people.

More research is needed to understand how magnetic and electrical energy activates chemical processes in the body. However, there is increasing evidence that these energies can be used to affect health effects.

So far, here's what we learned.

What are we aware of vibrations?

Vibration is a sort of rhythm. Rhythms occur on a wide scale, such as seasonal shifts and mare patterns. They even occur in your body.

Heartbeats, breathing and circadian patterns demonstrate the physiological rhythms that can be seen, felt, and measured.

But there are also much smaller movements in your body. Molecules vibrate at characteristic frequencies inside each of your cells.

Researchers observed nanoscale vibrations using atomic force microscopes—much less than one 1/1000th of the diameter of a single human hair.

These vibrations emit electromagnetic waves of energy. Researchers found that vibrations and the resulting electromagnetic radiation cause changes in your cells, which can influence the function of your body.

Different molecules vibrate at different rates and can speed up or slow down if molecular conditions change.

Temperature, for instance, can affect the vibration speed of a molecule.

How do feelings, actions and vibrations relate?

Researchers have long recognized that thoughts and conduct influence the body's rhythms.

Anxious thoughts, for example, activate the release of stress hormones that stimulate or slow your heart rate. The music's sound effects influence feelings, emotions and body systems as well.

Vibrational energy experts believe that our attitudes and emotions can also change rhythms far smaller.

Proponents assume that vibrations on cell and atomic levels can be accelerated or slowed down by modifying our feelings, actions and even the environment.

It is thought that changing these Nano vibrations could rip out to affect our mental and physical condition.

What are the advantages of vibratory energy?

Evidence suggests that the mind and body are closely linked.

The vibrational energy is not yet known as it blends into the relationship between both. Proponents think you should adjust the vibrations of your body to:

• Modify your mood
• Enhance your physical fitness
• Help you fulfil your objectives and purposes

Vibrational energy experts believe that certain emotions and patterns of thinking, such as joy, harmony and acceptance, produce high-frequency vibrations while others (such as despair, fear and anger) are slightly less vibrant.

There is no proof to support this connection. There is, however, plenty of evidence to relate positive emotions and thought habits to better health and a better objective.

Researchers found that vibrations of many kinds – electromagnetic, sound and light – can be used to induce cure and development in the body.

How do I adjust my energy of vibration?

Vibrational energy experts suggest various methods to boost the vibrations in the body and life.

While further research is needed to understand whether and how vibratory energy affects these activities, many of the suggested practices provide significant health benefits.

Breath work

The advocates suggest that deep rhythmic breathing is indeed a good way to adjust your vibratory capacity.

Research indicates that steady, regulated respiration will calm your heart rate and stimulate your brain's areas:

• Comfort
• Relaxation
• Emotional control
• Well-being

Meditation

In general, meditation includes sitting or sitting in a quiet zone, concentrating your attention on sensations of the body or on a given the word or object and allowing for your responses to alter while meditating.

Studies have indicated that, during rhythmic singing of the "Om" syllable, the vibration produced momentarily disables the amygdala and other brain structures involved in the emotional treatment.

Research indicates that meditation may also be:
- Change the pressure in your blood
- Reduce your vulnerability to pain
- influence your mood

Vibrational energy is also thought to help relieve the symptoms of:
- Irritable bowel syndrome
- Anxiety
- Insomnia
- Depression

Gratitude

It is also recommended to make time to note and appreciate what is positive in your life to lift your vibrations.

Health experts agree that they should show appreciation deliberately and regularly:
- Improve the psychological well-being
- Lower stress
- make you more likely to engage in physical fitness activities

Freedom

Generosity is designed to increase vibratory energy because it is considered a pro-social behaviour.

There is evidence that kindness will help you live longer, in addition to its potential impact on your vibratory capacity.

A 2013 study showed that kindness could extend your life by defending you against the damaging effects of stress.

Diet

Vibrational proponents of energy claim that it is vital to eat foods with higher levels of energy.

Note that no study has been carried out to measure vibration in food groups and that many of these foods are merely important for their health benefits.

Vibrational energy activists propose to increase vibrational energy by providing a diet rich in the following foods, linked to various health benefits:

- Leafy green vegetables
- Legumes
- Fresh fruits
- Minimally processed grains
- Spring water
- Honey
- Herbal teas

Vibrational energy supporters also say that the following foods should not consider themselves to have valuable vibrational energy and could also have adverse health effects:

- Meat
- Poultry
- Fish
- Alcohol
- fried foods
- Dairy
- Heavily processed food

Outdoor immersion

Go out into nature as much as possible to boost or reset your vibrational force.

You are assumed to be benefited from exposure to natural sound waves, light waves, negative ions and green spaces.

Multiple experiments have shown that nature interacts:

- lowers stress and blood pressure
- reduces fatigue
- reduces cortisol levels
- can reduce your risk of cardiovascular and breathing diseases

A stroll in the woods or a picnic next to a high-energy waterfall can also increase your cognitive function and well-being.

Healing Touch, therapeutic touch and Reiki

These three approaches are energy therapies. This allows a professional therapist to use a hands-on approach to transfer the energy in your body to enhance your health.

These therapies have been typically used for decades alongside other traditional medical procedures.

Specialists in vibrational energy suggest them to correct the flow of energy in and around the body.

Yoga

Yoga puts together the advantages of breathing, meditation, and rhythm.

There have been no studies on the impact of yoga on your vibrational energy.

However, multiple studies show that rhythmic yoga practice improves the scale, function, and connectivity of brain structures that are dedicated to your cognitive abilities.

Yoga was also shown:

• Enhance blood sugar levels
• Support for muscle and bone regeneration
• Enhance cardiovascular wellbeing
• Relieve anxiety and depression symptoms

Healthy connections

Energy experts agree that sound relationships increase vibrations, while conflict has the opposite effect.

The National Institutes of Health study the "strong impact" of your relationships on your health.

If you want to increase your environment, lower your stress and live longer and healthier lives, a network of relationships is important.

Family, family members, neighbours, colleagues and other social relations are required to:

- Express your concerns
- Facilitate conversations in the brain
- Immerse your life in the sense of self-respect and belonging.

Are there choices for vibrational energy?

In addition to the above practices, you may want to know more about other integrative and complementary alternative medical treatments.

Each therapy is partly focused on improving the flow of energy into your mind and body:

- Acupuncture
- Ayurveda medicine
- Qi gong
- Chakra therapy
- Polarity therapy
- PEMF (pulsed electromagnetic fields) therapy
- Sound Healing & Grounding

When do I see a physician?

Rising vibrational energy will bring good health benefits, but it should not be used to treat mental or physical problems on its own.

It's crucial to seek traditional treatments along with integrative or complementary therapies if you have physical, mental or emotional symptoms that affect your qualities of life.

Talk to a health professional about how vibrational energy therapy can be combined with a tailored medication to alleviate the symptoms and cure any underlying health problems.

The molecular vibrations in your body can be tiny, but they can have a seismic impact on your health.

Energy medicine is increasing. If you would like to enhance your understanding of how energy and vibration affect your health, contact an integrative medicine professional in your field.

Although there is little research to understand the benefits and disadvantages of vibrational energy, many vibrational energy methods provide well-researched benefits for health.

Deep respiration, meditation, yoga and meditation will increase your vibrational energy. It may also help to communicate with nature, eat a healthy diet, and develop good ties and practice appreciation and kindness.

If you want to collaborate with a health care provider to increase your vibe, it may be good choices for a Reiki or Therapeutic Contact practitioner.

<u>Love Yourself, Love Your Body</u>

Many people assume that they would be inspired to do something about themselves if they are very crazy and annoy themselves for being overweight. You know that if you tried this technique, it doesn't work. It just causes you to feel worse. What works is to love yourself and your body and to accept that you don't have to change something. You are fine right now - regardless of the scales or mirror or the size of your clothing. To achieve and control your weight, love yourself and embrace yourself as you are.

Nothing's wrong with you. The only problem is that you think something is wrong with you. If you consider yourself to be bad, lower or missing, it reduces your vibration and blocks the object of your wish. Dressing your body is a low vibration that sends a signal that repels, excludes and prevents your ideal body from appearing. When you change the way you talk, the body reflects this progress positively.

When she was a teenager, Florence was overweight all her life and diet. Now in her fifties, she had health issues, and her doctor advised that she would lose at least 60 or her health would get worse. Florence could never adhere to a diet and was afraid to lose her health. Then she discovered that the trick is to change her way of thinking and to talk to herself. She started to say that she loves and appreciates herself. She began to regard herself as a precious human. She started referring to herself with dignity and completely REFUSED to let anyone talk to her. With this vibrational change in her thoughts and emotions, Florence could lose her weight, recover her health, and for the first time ever, really enjoy her life.

Take it from Florence and replace yourself with love and kindness. You have a choice to love, admire and judge yourself. Speak to yourself about how you relate to your best friend. Take note of your internal dialogue and select ideas that make you feel good.

Substitute negative self-talk:

- Something is wrong with me.
- If I look as society tells me that, I'm not good enough.
- Nobody's going to love me if I don't look fine.
- I still can't get what I want.

With self-speech empowerment:
- I'm awesome. - My look pleases my eyes.
- My body is just as beautiful as it is.
- My personality is exciting and attractive.
- I just love myself as I am.
- I'm flattering about my clothes.
- I love my life. - I love my life.
- I love my body. I love my body.
- My deeds are kind and compassionate.

You relate to the natural state of well-being when you love yourself and your body. When you love your body as it is now, you resist and allow your body to comply with your desires. Your thoughts have produced the body that you have now. Your thoughts will build the body that you want.

Raise Your Vibration - Raise Your Thought - Raise Your Life!

By controlling your emotions and not allowing negative things, you increase your vibration, your energy level by increasing the flow of positive energy in your inner world! Your outside world will then reflect this to you through increased cash flow, better relationships, more resources, better health and more imaginative, happy experiences!

Mirror on the Wall!
Anything you're thinking about and believing can, don't doubt it, it's the way the world works, and don't you believe it? Look, think of it, think of your life? What do you feel in your everyday life? Are you happy? Are you pleased? What don't you like? What do you not like? So how did it happen? Really think how this thing you don't like might have appealed to your world. What are your thoughts and feelings about the situation? Change them!
Your world continuously represents your emotions, feelings, behaviours and your concentration. If you're not pleased with anything, it's hard to think negative, and it's hard not to think all the time!

So, ow are we changing this!

What you always think is your truth, so don't think about what you don't like. Find out how you can turn the situation into a positive experience and concentrate on it! Just think about what you want!
The images & thoughts in your mind are mirrored back to you, creating real results which you will feel physically. Guaranteed!
Get your mind firmly, and then you cannot go wrong, as soon as you really realize that it is what you think, feel and believe creates your life, you can make it like magic. Remember to constantly just imagine what you want! If you concentrate on the positive outcome of what your heart wants only, the universe is compelled to start physically to give you this wish.
You have a good mind!
You're a strong being who can show what you want in your life, so get to work, stop wasting your life, and live the lives of your dreams! If you don't build and manifest what you really want in life constantly, you are flying in the face of the Universe! You deny yourself!
Just make your choice today to make a big difference in your way of thinking, thinking and feeling! Take your life back by seeing how strong you are.
When we are scary and pessimistic, we will attract more of the same in our lives; if we worry about what we don't want, can you see that we will never be free until we decide to be free?

It's worth being free!

We all merit fear and pain, and we merit the best; we merit happiness, but only if we make a choice!

Make your choice today to be alive, to be happy and to have all you want. All we need to do is accept and live this idea. It. take some time to remove the old patterns but make the option! When we live at this higher level of vibration and take responsibility, we live with joy, appreciation, affection, independence and confidence every day, attracting positive circumstances and results with uncomfortable ease. Learn to live with a higher vibration, embrace your strength and put into your life everything you want. It's just as simple as making the decision. So today, you want the life in which you imagine, don't dream it, and live it! My success to you, to everything you deserve and want!

This vibration increase sequence to allow you to live with more energy, fitness, love, happiness, wisdom and abundance, so you can become a strong, positive and transformative force in our world. In Part One, we have discussed Step One to increase your energy charge and increase the amount of energy you have. If you're exhausted and weary, you have no energy and no energy to cultivating a higher frequency.

Step Two is to identify and release the pressures which interfere with this energy's smooth and joyful flow.

Life is Renewal, Movement, and Change

Life is movement, regeneration, and transition. Nothing is the same. Nothing is the same. All come up, grows, lingers and fades. Our bodies die as we stop moving, renovating and evolving. Every moment is fresh, and every moment is new. Each cell in your body replaces every 7-10 years and renews much faster than that.

However, when we are afraid of events, we wish to avoid the flow of life. We want to shut down stuff. We freeze or delete. We search for protection from the emotional storm and try to stop it from running.

"Life is secure if I only stick to what I know, who I know, and places I know, instead of going further." We try to determine situations in ways that make them less frightening. We strive to describe ourselves as "I'm not nice, so I won't try" in ways that keep us safe. We identify comfort zones of thinking, activity, relationship and defence against change. We're trying to keep things as they are.

We then adhere to these strictly established limits of ourselves, relationships and events as if our lives depend on them. This causes stress in our minds and bodies. We harden these stresses and harden them to life. We are losing our receptiveness to change and diversity within ourselves and others and our ability to evolve, cure and renovate. Our desire to "go with the flow" is lost.

Let's discuss how these stresses can be recognized and relieved so that we can recover our capacity to live in grace and compassion. This is the second step towards elevating our vibration.

The main flows in your body

Let's use the blood flow example to better understand the role of flow. The blood flow through our bodies is vital to life. The blood flow leads all our cells to oxygen and nutrients and removes toxins from our cells. Our bodies die in minutes without blood supply.

However, several activities impede blood flow—stress and trauma restricting the normal complete breathing, leading to blood vessel constriction. Chronic strain, as well as toxins and some foods and beverages, increases inflammation, leading to scar, plaque formation and less sensitivity of the blood vessels. Emotions like fear, worry, and anxiety produce muscle and connective tissue stress that prevents blood flow to muscles and inner bodies. They cannot get oxygen and nutrients and cannot release toxins when this occurs. These cells become hungry and toxic. They can't renew and start a slow death anymore.

Life in our bodies, therefore, includes blood-free flow, lymph fluid free flow, nerve signals and physical motion. The nature of life is smooth flow, and stress limits this flow. To boost flow, stress must be established and released so that these natural flows are reverted. When and where tension occurs, our bodies signal us, so if we pay attention, we can take steps to understand and alleviate these tensions.

However, these stresses are so natural for most of us that we don't even know that they're there. Fortunately, we will learn about their symptoms and understand them.

Tension Identification
By these signs, you can identify inner tension:

• Congestion
• Indigestion
• Muscle pain and stiffness
• Headache
• Feeling stuck
• Brain fog and confusion
• Anxiety and worry
• Difficulty breathing
• Restricted movement
• Chronic Fatigue
• Emotional overwhelm
• Angry outbursts, agitation, irritation
• Depression
• Chronic illness
• Addictions
• Harsh judgments of self and others
• Repeated poor results in your finances, life, and relationships.

You might look at the list and say, "This covers almost every issue I may have. Can any of these be attributed to tension?"

"Yes," is the answer?

Tensions in your body, mind, and emotions impede the smooth flow of your system's blood, lymph, nerve signals and life energy.

So, how do you understand the stress and relieve it?
This is a straightforward but efficient process you can use.

Steps to identify and release internal tensions

1. Pause any sign of tension, pain, frustration or discomfort when you encounter any of the above.

Let go of the anxiety surrounding it for a moment. See for a moment if you can let it go and make it bigger. Let go of some stories for a moment that your mind would like to tell where those symptoms would lead.

2. Be careful of the body's sensations, with interest and non-judgment. Note the qualities thought. Is the pain in your body specific? Has this area a scale, shape, colour, texture and intensity? There was a mistake.

3. Cause the environment to have a sense of space. Allow this room to extend in all directions, so the room feels big, and the stress area is small. Imagine compassion in this vacuum.

4. Ask the spacious area from your point of view if it has anything to say to you.

See if you can just float this query, listen and feel without hastening to receive a response. Note whatever comes up, whether it's thinking, feeling, image, and feeling.

5. Gently allow the tense area to embrace, infuse, and calm the caring spaciousness around it. When you inhale, imagine and feel as if you breathe love and compassion into the tense zone. When you exhale, imagine and believe that you expel the stress from your body.

Continue to breathe until you have clarity, feel relaxed and/or experience a difference in what is going on.

These steps start a time-consuming healing process. You will need to repeat this process with the same area or problem several times, especially if the stress lasts a long time or refers to dominant thinking, feeling, beliefs you have maintained for a long time.

Take this activity into account as part of your everyday routine so that you release stress layers that have been stored in your life. This way to check the bodysuits well with prayer/meditation in the morning or evening and is also effective as a timeout in the middle of tough times throughout the day.

When you regularly use these measures over time, your body begins to feel looser, lighter and freer. You're going to be happier, empowered, and alive! Your energy and consciousness will increase. You will be able to flow with life, be encouraged and directed by the current, and adapt fluently and gracefully to changes. You will begin to live in a higher frequency of presence, compassion and understanding in the interests of all beings and all our world.

******

"Knowing Yourself Is the Beginning of All Wisdom."

~ Aristotle

CHAPTER TWO

<u>What Is Your Emotional Status?</u>

You should be emotionally intelligent and know yourself in many respects. It can be brilliant, sophisticated, humorous, and you can even manage those situations well. Often you can wonder why you can't get it right. Perhaps all your relationships have ended the same or the same complaint. This may be a lack of emotional intelligence. This factor is an important factor in a good relationship.

Do you understand your feelings? Do you understand? Second, you must realize why you feel what you are doing. Are you sticking to pass wrath? Do you assume the result? Do you treat every feeling in the same way? Both can lead to emotional confusion, which can be prevented. Make a step in the right direction to concentrate your emotions on the situation. Do not allow any feeling to get the best of yourself. Take a breath or take a moment alone.

Now, you understand why you feel positive in some way. I typically create a journal of constructive thinking for my customers. It's something that helps you start every day and keep you positive. If your feelings are constructive, you can better evaluate yourself and the emotions of others. Keeping negative from your thinking is a crucial factor in a happier life.

Once you grasp your emotions and think good thoughts down, you need to know how to efficiently control your emotions. Learn how to cope with problems rather than respond to them—controlling the need for explosion or mental disintegration. These items will help you effectively and efficiently react to emotions. Express and share how you feel with your romantic partner. Checks and checks are often important for love. It goes a long way to say basic things or gestures. "I love you." "I love you." "I value you." "I love you." "How's your day been?"

"Something I can bring you?" These basic things let others know that you care. Expression of love and compassion does not have to be grandiose to help people understand how they feel.

By combining these elements, you will begin to increase your level of emotional intelligence. In addition to raising your E-I level, all your relationships, especially intimate ones, will improve. Relationships are a large part of life and effort to make them meaningful. Relationships don't have to be a tough job, but we just make them out of habit at times.

Emotional intelligence will transform your life. You will have stronger connections if you take easy regular steps to evaluate yourself. Learn verbal and nonverbal indications, how feelings should be handled and not suppressed. Understanding how and how you feel will create a happier atmosphere.

<u>Emotional Intelligence for Getting What You Want</u>

Your emotional intelligence guides the course of your life. It creates your "luck", and it has the power to give you something or to take it all away. The thoughts and feelings you focus on through your creative mind are the commands which bring with them the power of change in your life. These brainwave signals communicate with the world, and through the law of attraction, give you MORE of what your viewpoint is gazing upon. This infinite force is operating at any moment of your life that if you're not aware of it. The good news is that you are in charge, or rather, you can be if you like.

Choose to take responsibility for your life's thoughts and sentiments now, and you will have allowed your dreams to manifest!

Classify your feelings and prepare yourself to understand them. There are "positive" feelings and "negative" feelings, right? If you know what they are? Of course, you do! Then why do so many people waste so much of their time focusing on problems that make them feel bad? Does this help the good feelings return? Many individuals apparently go out of their way to feel bad by their consistent negative thoughts and behaviours, yet they wonder why so many bad things happen to them! Good or poor, whatever emotion generating thoughts you saturate your mind with and thus send out to the world, you will get more of back in return. This is how you "feel" to others, to yourself, to your circumstances and to everything in between. Identify unwanted feelings in your life that lead to stressful events. Just by being aware of the effect your emotions have, your emotional intelligence can go a long way.

You can choose your ideas and regulate your emotions. Understanding the clear and powerful fact that what you feel later gives you an insight into how your life can be better. Your emotional intelligence totally depends on building the knowledge and mental habit of thinking about your emotions. Have you ever had a beautiful day, and anything "out of the blue" would spoil it? Or have you ever begun a Monday off with something terrible, another bad thing followed, and so on until "the bad snowball of the events becomes one of those days?" We all witnessed this, but here's the key you missed, you asked!

By reflecting on what made you feel bad, you asked for more emotion! And then you were given more reasons for feeling bad, what you commanded! Nearly every negative experience can be traced to the same negative feelings before they occur! Just like enthusiasm and joy are felt before we do something that makes us feel like that. What you must always remember and keep with you is that your perspective and concentration define how you feel about something. And this "mind-set" feeling determines your mood, and it builds your future!

Do not take your mind as a matter of course. Your feelings are strong arms tools and emotions that you can use to support or harm yourself. Emotional intelligence means that nothing, thing or occurrence will ever govern your life in luxury.

It means taking responsibility for mistakes of the past and forgiving yourself for them and those that hurt you. It means staying optimistic and deciding how you feel about yourself, irrespective of what another person tries to tell you. When you just think about things that make you feel good, you draw more into your life! This is true of any emotion we want and even of those we don't want. Envy will offer more causes for envy. Frustration is going to create stressful situations. Joy is going to offer reasons for celebration! And thanks, fill your life with joy and abundance!

You can find reasons at any moment to celebrate or lament. Both are still there and what you're focusing on is what comes to life. The strength of your inner appreciation is equivalent to your emotional intelligence. What you are grateful for is multiplied in your life. There is no better way to express it or to change your life. Stop feeling guilty and moaning about what's hurting you! Do not expect another human or higher power to "save" you simply because you are good at making yourself miserable. This behaviour is like a child who thinks if he throws his fit dramatically enough, someone will fix his problem.

They have the power to do it all the time! You, too, have access to the most efficient, unlimited and innovative resource available for universal energy. This energy functions within the law of attraction and are driven by the ideas and feelings that you command. See now in your life the many reasons you need to be thankful and feel it with all your heart! Only this workout, and nothing else, is enough to improve your life!

Measures are often better than reactions. Stop responding to life. Try to pause before any new emotions or mood to see whether it's a positive or a negative sensation first. If it is a bad feeling, choose to concentrate your thinking on what you love most.

If you can't find a good spin right now, only find a reason to feel thankful, and another and the other until your happiness outweighs the bad circumstance that passes. This is an example of functioning emotional intelligence. Choosing the path and, therefore, the trajectory of their lives pro-actively. When your mental development grows, the possibilities of your future outline your circumstances. Offer life through the prism of love and in the light of appreciation to the true beauty of your successful world.

How to Raise Your Emotional Intelligence

You must become aware of the emotion that you are feeling at any moment in order to increase your emotional intelligence level and must also deal with the feelings that you have hidden in order to avoid coping with them. It is a common inclination to force down or to tell yourself you don't have a certain emotion because it's painful or because under conditions, the emotion appears inappropriate. Emotional intelligence allows you to know and control your own emotions.

It's not something you can do automatically - it's an operation. To complete this step successfully, it helps you recall the following details about your emotions:

Emotional understanding is dependent on emotional consciousness.

Emotional intelligence is different from normal or classic intelligence since you can literally at will increase your emotional intelligence. And being emotionally intelligent is an important element in establishing strong relationships with family, friends and colleagues. People with a high degree of emotional intelligence are valued because they are stable, calm, and confident and seem to have the inherent ability to understand others. They seem to still know what to do in any situation because they are not overwhelmed by their feelings so that they can think clearer and act more rational.

Emotions are constantly changing.

Becoming conscious of and what stimulates your feelings isn't the same as living on them. Take note of how one emotion and another emotion will emerge in the various things you do on a given day, and you will find that emotions are often subject to change.

Your feelings are also linked to your physical feeling.

You've probably noticed that the way your body responds to the fearful feeling is different from the happiness emotion, that when you're glad, you feel physically different from when you're upset, etc. Take care that your hands shake, your muscles are tight, and your heart struck quickly, both of which are bound to be afraid, and help you understand why you are afraid so that you can treat that fear constructively.

Emotional intelligence is not a substitute for reason and logic.

Being mindful of what feelings and emotions you experience and learning how to handle these emotions and feelings will essentially become automatic. When you no longer try unconsciously to control your emotions and feelings, you're reasoning and thinking skills are simpler and more precise, and you can use them to work through your emotions without them being overcome. Just like everything else, you get better by training and practicing.

When we understand our feelings, what they are and how they affect us, we construct the foundations for self-consciousness. Self-control then takes the direction of increasing our emotional intelligence with a different set of competencies.

WAYS TO RAISE YOUR VIBRATION

You can improve your emotional state or vibration in several ways. Here we talk about a few that can support you.

1. You must follow your nose

Some essential oils can change your emotional condition very quickly just by having a deep whiff. These can be found easily in health food or in some spiritual shops. You can then test and buy the fragrances that pip you.

2. Stress on Appreciation and Gratitude

Thanksgiving impacts mood tremendously. You just must concentrate on something that in life you are incredibly grateful for and note your increase on several levels—even easier appreciation. You can just walk around your house and look at stuff and feel love for all of them. Easier to drive around; just look at your environment and people and enjoy them all.

3. Make it a habit to hear the music

Music is like a fragmented one and can give you an instant elevation. You only have to select a form of music that lifts you and brings you into a higher state.

4. Just Get Out and Touch Someone

You will find it incredible how nice you feel when you just turn your focus to something else. So, you just need to call someone, be a relative or friend and feel the connection!

5. Get busy having fun with your pet

Cats can be really amusing and can keep you from tension for the time you spend with them. Likewise, dogs can be very fun. Take your day out for this fun walk, or just play with your dog for a while.

6. Walk in Nature

You must go to this little paradise. You will understand nature in ways you never saw before. Sunshine, exercise, all these are perfect vibrational raisers.

7. Relaxation always does something that you would want to do

It's playing the organ for others. You will soon be engulfed in this. You never feel stressed when you do something you want to do.

If You Wish to Be Happier, Raise Your Emotional Intelligence

Were you aware that Emotional Intelligence (EQ) is much more predictive than your IQ? In this section, you'll find out what Emotional Intelligence is, how to get rid of it, and the first step towards making your EQ happier.

Most of us know the calculation of intelligence according to the well-known cognitive intelligence IQ classification. Dr. Howard Gardner of Harvard University suggested in 1983 that this number is at best a partial measure. He suggested eight different forms of intelligence: linguistic, mathematical-logical, spatial, bodily-kinaesthetic, artistic, interpersonal, intrapersonal and natural intelligence. In other words, we can be smart beyond I.Q. Steps in important ways.

The field of multiple intelligences has since vanished. Recently, Emotional Intelligence (EQ) has been the number one indicator of professional and personal achievement and satisfaction in life.

Researchers identify a number.

Four Emotional Intelligence Skills Essential:

1. Self-consciousness: capacity to perceive your thoughts and tendencies correctly.

2. Self-management: the ability to use your emotional consciousness to be resilient and to guide your behaviour.

3. Social awareness: the ability to perceive and understand other people's emotions.

4. Control of relationships: the ability to use the consciousness of your own thoughts and feelings for successful interpersonal interactions.

Fortunately, as opposed to I.Q., which seems innate and unchanging, EQ is something that is learned and improved. However, a quick look at the news shows that EQ is inadequate. We, therefore, see highly divided experiences causing discord, tension, anxiety and suspicion. Why doesn't emotional intelligence seem to be so necessary that we can master it?

Why do you elude us with emotional intelligence?

We live in a culture that does not understand the purpose of feeling and encourages us to disregard feelings in favour of "doing things." Ironically, the very feelings we neglect are what stops us from getting things done, understanding what is important to do, and working well with others.

Emotions provide us with guidance on what really happens in our relationships with others. Skilfully handled, they allow us to establish boundaries, relate effectively to others and interact with what is important for our own lives. Every emotion is used to a and indispensable function, according to Karla McLaren (author of the 'Language of Emotions').

However, from our earliest years, we have been encouraged to be too emotional. We are told that there are positive and bad emotions. In most cases, we are told that "putting a happy face" is best.

It is OK and justifiable to feel frustration only in specific circumstances. In some cases, we can be sad, but not for too long. We can never dwell on feelings of remorse or disgrace, conquer fear and envy, and never experience hatred. This is understandable given the pain caused throughout human history by the unconscious and untrained manifestation of these emotions.

Wrath and hate are synonymous with bigotry, bullying and aggression. We equate depression with sorrow. We equate jealousy with the conflict between people. Fear is associated with repression. We do not care about apathy. We combine negative emotions with unqualified manifestations of these feelings, and we strive to stop them.

Not only is negative emotion to stop, but even positive exuberance is deemed to be too sweet. We are expected to be calm, cool and composed, no matter what we really feel inside, except in those circumstances where the excitement is encouraged, like parties or sporting events.

Due to our uneasiness with emotions in general and negative emotions, we become experts in three activities which distract, avoid and addict emotions.

1. Distance.
    You are told to distract yourself from your childhood. Who did not hold a sweet stuffed toy and make dumb noises to distract a baby from crying? As an adult, you can keep yourself from understanding your feelings with television, work or "to-do lists."

2. Avoidance
    Avoidance is a more deliberate rejection of your sentiments. You repress them instead. When you inquire for an emotional answer, you say, "I'm all right. I'm good. It's nothing. I'm fine." Eventually, this habit leads to mental numbness and a lack of sensation in acute circumstances.

3. Addiction.
    Addiction, by repeating an action that generates a different biochemical reaction, you dissociate from a specific feeling. You drink caffeine, for example, to dissociate yourself from weariness, shyness, or sorrow; drink alcoholic drinks to stupor feelings of grief, tension, frustration, or pain; excessive exercise to replace depression with high endorphin or eat to suppress feelings of emptiness. It's not that all these behaviours themselves are "negative." This is how you use them to support or hurt them.

Each of us has preferred dissociative behaviours, and sometimes they are required. You need a break from intense emotions often or simply cannot carry out an exhausting event at any time. But if dissociation is a persistent habit and you do not recognize and learn from your emotions, that is an issue.

If you repeatedly ignore signals in your emotions, you cut off the key thread of contact between your consciousness and the deeper currents of your life. You detach from your inner guidance, which can help you be healthier, happier, more integrated, deliberate and alive. Taking your emotions off often separates you from emotional contact with others, which is the foundation for deeper and more loving relationships.

Emotional Intelligence Growing

So, what do you do? What can you do? How can you switch this around and start your emotional intelligence to grow?

The first step is to pay more attention to your emotions by perceiving what your body feels. Before you hit the television remotely, you will notice the sensations of emotion as you snack, coffee, and alcohol or pain medication.

Ask yourself, "Where would it be if this sensation were anywhere in my body?" Then characterize it as a physical feeling. Is it cold, hot? Is there strain or tightness? Numbness? Itching? Nausea? Nausea? Development? Is contraction a contraction? Rising? Sinking?

Although these sensations may seem like a weird thing to do, particularly if they feel awkward, to be happier, this is the first step towards connection with emotional guidance. In these feelings, there is a deeper awareness. Paying attention to emotional stimuli is a way to access, observe and educate you.

When you're in contact with the feeling, ask yourself, "What's the message?" Notice what's in mind.

It is important to bear in mind that emotions are temporary if you are reluctant to deal with emotions. It doesn't feel forever. They come up with a reason. When you are present, an emotion gives you details about what is happening inside, around you and through the motivation of others to do things. Once emotional advice is considered, it falls.

Attracting Wealth - Raising Your Vibration is Key

It is easy to attract wealth through the rule of attraction when you know how to live. However, it is not easy because we always think and behave in exactly the opposite way because our mind conditioning is complicated, but it can be entirely possible for anyone. All have a vibration in this world. This involves emotions, feelings and even the chair in which you sit. When people talk about attracting wealth and the law of attraction, they hear more about vibrations. That's because it's the vibrations that decide what you draw. Good items have strong vibrations and poor vibrations.

Consider the variations between the thoughts and feelings when in a good mood rather than a negative one.

Or when you feel well rather than sick in bed. When you attract money, you obviously need to have good pictures of your wishes, statements and intentions, feel rich, irrespective of outside conditions, and have confidence and belief that you have already earned what you want. These are the biggest as far as the law of attraction is concerned.

In this post, I want to explore some other methods of maintaining a high vibration that does not necessarily equate with money and stuff that you are looking for. These are the keys, of course, but too often, as soon as they do their meditation, people go back to their old ways or put down the book for the day or end their visualizations and affirmations. It is not enough to feel good when doing your visualizations and then fall back into your old way of thinking five minutes later. You need to improve your life and break some bad habits in order to achieve the highest vibration to attract wealth. Below are three things that have made a big difference in my life, and I know that for you, this will be the same thing.

1. Do not use Terms for yourself or anyone.

This is a biggie. This is a biggie. At a time or another, every one of us guilty of gossip. It's like a drug flowing through our veins. It helps us feel better at judging others or seeing others with issues, and it makes us feel more comfortable with ourselves and our lives.

It can make us feel better than others. But the funny thing is you've ever noticed how you have felt during a chat session, spoken to others and made assumptions about their behaviour and decisions? It's awful. It's a low pulse, and it's just a lot of negativities that doesn't help the objectives. It is never our place to criticize or be catty and say something about their weight, clothing or something else. To chatter and speak out against others is to label your life as insecure and miserable. You cannot get it by thinking poorly about other people if you want to draw money and positive things into your life. Stop talking about how others live their lives and concentrate on your own. Next time you talk to others, take note of the environment and do your best to refrain.

The same is true for speaking out against you. Next time someone compliments you, don't counteract them. Just say, thank you. There is nothing wrong with trusting and knowing what you do and what you are good at. Do not bring yourself down. Modesty certainly has its position, but we are so bound to always understand ourselves, and it is nonsense. It is very difficult to attract wealth if you have a poor opinion of yourself.

2. Fill your mind with positive information that contributes to your goals and decrease bad information.

You can hear it all the time but reduce or remove your negative intake. Newspapers, night news and 24-hour news stations are some of the main reasons for low vibration. It's sometimes so subtle that you don't even know how profoundly it affects you. Sure, I understand that I want to be aware of major events in the world, but much of what you see in the news doesn't help you, and you simply know nothing about another rape, murder or the killing of your child by your parents. Furthermore, if you buy into all this, all the "poor economy" talk will drive wealth from you more quickly than anything else. External conditions have little to do with personal achievement. Please know this. Please know this. Although we're not talking about such healthy mental food, you have to reduce the amount of television you watch. Most of it is waste and will not help you to attract wealth. Insipid reality shows and all junk is the lowest type of entertainment, and if you spend most of your free time outside the TV, I can assure you that you will not have true success in life, especially financially. There is nothing wrong with any shows you like. Just pick them carefully. If you don't read at least a few books a month on attraction rule, wealth attraction and other self-development subjects, you must start now. Our programming is so far removed. The only way to reprogram is by constantly reinforcing books, CD's, lectures, and so on. If you have a person who thinks like that in your life, count yourself fortunate and speak to them as much as you can. If you want to attract money, you will need to feed your mind better and invest your time more wisely.

3. Engage your physical well-being.

Mind and body are closely interconnected, and that becomes more evident with time. One of the best ways to improve the pulse is to make you feel comfortable physically and mentally, eat well, meditate and participate in other activities. You don't need to train like an Olympian, but if you don't train and eat well at present, I can guarantee you that you don't vibrate as high as you can. Start easy and build up your path. Stop the excuses "I don't have time." You can find foe like 30 minutes a few days a week when you give up some TV.

As I said above, the visualizations that concentrate on needs and wishes, etc., form the cornerstones of attracting wealth and the law of attraction, but you need to add some resources to your arsenal to keep it as much as possible throughout the day, to sustain the highest vibration. The above three aspects will change enormously if you make a deliberate effort to integrate them into your life.

******

"What You Think You Become,
What You Feel You Attract,
What You Imagine You Create."

~ Buddha

CHAPTER THREE

<u>Law of Attraction - How to Raise Manifesting Vibration</u>

A high vibration enhances the ability to manifest. If you look at the voltage of a battery as vibration, just assume that the higher the voltage, the higher the power the battery can emit. The same applies to your own condition if you can think and sense a higher voltage.

You can hold a powerful vibration easier by watching and then elevating your emotions. Since your thoughts often precede your emotions, you first need to realize the quality of your thoughts before they become negative feelings.

This is not to suggest you should be mad for any negative thinking you have. However, for your spiritual growth, it is important for you to learn to lift your thoughts purposefully when they sink into doom and dullness.

One of the first moves you can take is to put several questions to your elves. Not only can you control your own inner self, but your capacity to manifest will increase.

Here are a few questions you would like to ask yourself when your thoughts sink:

- Am I the only person to deal with this problem?
- How did others deal with this issue?
- What will it feel when I overcome this problem?
- What stages can I take now to facilitate this problem?

These questions will certainly trigger your mind to move from what you don't want to do. Manifestation is a knowledge of the mind that needs experience. The stronger your vibration, the more you train the mind to locate higher thoughts and feelings, the easier it gets to attract what you want.

<u>How to Raise Your Vibration by Using Aromatherapy and Color Therapy?</u>

You may mix a complementary pair of colours, such as yellow and violet or pink and green, to produce a perfect combination of Aromatherapy with Color vibration. You may also use Color as a method of using essential oils by combining oils with identical or additional colours.

Orange skin tonic

Put in 1/2 cup/4 fl. oz. /100 ml orange floral water, 16 drops of orange oil and four drops of neroli. Use as a cleaner, if necessary. Do not use if pregnant. Do not use. Do not leave for at least 72 hours in the heat.

Violet/Yellow Healing Balm for Spots and Acne

Mix two drops of essential lemon oil and a drop of essential lavender with six drops of primrose oil in the evening. Spread morning and evening over the affected area. Do not leave for at least 72 hours in the heat. Do not use it if you are pregnant.

Blemished Skin with Violet Tonic

In ½ cup/4 fl. oz/100 ml. of lavender water, add 12 drops of lavender and clean the affected area. Do not use it while pregnant. Do not use.

Bath Mix Red / Yellow Cellulite

In 2 table cubes/30 ml, mix with Almond Oil. 2 drops of lemon and one drop of essential oil of sandalwood. Add to the bathroom as required.

- Red - Sandalwood
- White - Cajeput
- Gold - Patchouli
- Olive Green - Essential oils produced from herbs, Himalaya Pine.

- Yellow - Lemon, Citronella, Evening Primrose Oil, Lemongrass, Camphor
- Orange - Cinnamon, Orange, Carrot Seed Oil, Mandarin, Neroli
- Pink - Geranium
- Emerald Green - Rosemary, Basil, Scotch Pine, Peppermint
- Deep Magenta - Clary Sage, Frankincense
- Royal Blue - German Chamomile
- Sapphire Blue - Tea Tree, Myrrh, Roman Chamomile
- Violet - Rose, Violet, Lavender, Rose Geranium, Juniper

VIBRATIONAL ENERGY

Subtle energy is generated by the energy anatomy of our body, also known as our delicate anatomy. The body is encircled by a vibrational field, usually known as the aura. The aura is an electromagnetic force field, which circles and permeates all living things in both the animal and the plant kingdom. The force field covers the body and protects it. Maybe often you can see the light around a person's head, or you can feel the mood of someone. If so, you can become conscious of the field of human energy called the Aura. The colours of the aura indicate the personality, health and spirituality of the individual. The aura is multi-coloured, flowing and moving with you, changing Color with your moods, emotions and spirit.

Disease and disorder are physical diseases that are blocked or intruded by the body's energy flow or, in some cases, too free of flux in or near vital organs. The flow is disrupted or trapped, or imbalanced, by thought, which ultimately acts as a pain or an organic disorder of some kind in the physical body.

This is the real essence of diseases and disorders that are prone to humanity. The release of the healing forces relies on this specific phase of the cleaning, which can be cleaned using aromatherapy and Color therapy.

Aromatherapy

Important oils include needles, grasses, skins, pellets, trees, bark, leaves, seeds, herbs, berries, flowers, roots, fruit, flowers, forests, spices. Oils are obtained from nuts, spices, fruit kernels, beeswax, bulbs, flowering seeds, fruit seeds, trees, herbs, carriers that are carrying essential oils in the body and bloodstream. They are thicker to bear the essential oils in the body. Aromatherapy promotes body health, peace of mind, allows negative emotions to relax and helps a person to reach out to their true self by working with an olfactory system. Essential oils become a leading alternative to in-home care. Many chiropractors value essential oils with wonderful results in the treatment of chiropractic. Tones that stimulate the emotional centre of the brain and redefine psychology. Orthodox Indian Ayurvedic medicine practitioners have respected essential oils for thousands of years. More and more physicians are assessing the therapeutic advantages of essential oils. Aromatherapy is also used as a complement to key occupations such as nursing, geriatrics, recovery, counselling and physical therapy. Available in the fields of naturopaths, hospices, hospitals, special needs, leisure travel, spas, retreats and cruise ships, health centres. Aromatherapy is used in massages, compresses, baths, sitting baths, infusions, perfumes, facial care, and hair care. Hair treatments. They can be used by both humans and animals. Do not use essential oils on small livestock or cats.

The recognized physical and mental effects of essential oils also indicate their subtle properties. Rosemary, for instance, encourages mental clarity and alleviates tiredness. On a subtle level, Rosemary is closely linked to the sixth energy centre (Third Eye) and is used to inspire critical thinking and insight. The juniper is physically cleansing and antiseptic. It is used on a subtle level to purify a space of negativity and to detoxify the subtle bodies.

The Patch Test

If you are unsure how your skin will react to essential oil, put one drop of the oil into your bracelet or forearm. Test the spot after a few hours for any redness, itching, discomfort or discomfort. Or if it needs to be applied a few minutes before a massage.

You should cover it with a Band-Aid if you have very fragile skin and you want to be very careful and leave it for 24 hours. You may also use the same techniques for carriers.

Color Therapy

Color therapy is used in special needs centres for children. For children with learning disabilities, Color therapy is used. An individual child's coloured filter that is put over their reading material allows a child to learn more. The most common Color is yellow. Using blue light at bedtime allows children to relax and sleep and was used to comfort children with ATD.

Color is the small visible component of the large spectrum of electromagnetic energy that is one of the universe's fundamental powers. The light operates at the subatomic (quantum) stage and fills the whole region (as the microwave background radiation - an echo of the Big Bang of cosmic creation). All life on earth relies on the nutritional resources of sunlight, which is conveniently derived from the Earth's atmosphere of harmful ultraviolet radiation. Light, as bio-photons, also acts as a contact within the body's cells and outside the body to infuse the auric fields. The life and psychology of a person are symbolically linked to colours and colours in the aura.

You could "see red" or "feel blue." You may be 'in the dark' or shot with a vivid and enthusiastic spark. Growing spiritual consciousness is connected to pale teeth and the golden-white light, which unifies all colours and stands for the unity or source of all.

You may use Color by placing a coloured light bulb into a light and shining it on your own, or by breathing in Color, or by watching it. You can also position a Color filter around a glass of water and allow the sun to shine over it to make polarized water for a few hours. You can buy coloured filters from lighting companies. Then the water has the vibration of any Color filter you have placed around the bottle. Your whole system will share the Color effects and benefit from them. You may use a swing arm lamp to apply Color therapy.

In the centre of each square, you can cut out two carton squares with a giant square. Two pieces of this are required. Then you tape the two bits together. Leave an opening between the two pieces of the carton to slip in your coloured filters. Then the square at the base of your swing arm lamp would be Velcro. You can then either use coloured bulbs.

You can buy it from a lamp or hardware store. Or coloured filters may be used. When you do this, you shine or systemically shine the light on a body part. This means that you shine the sun for one hour at a time over the front or back of your body. Some Chroma Therapy (Color Therapy) programs teach that you do not shine purple light on the forehead. You should stay between various Color treatments for an hour or two. You should also do a dowse or a muscle test to see if the Color for that period is right. For lamp care, a person who is not comfortable under a certain Color should not use that Color. It's nice for you if you like Color. If you have a neutral Color reaction, you probably don't need it. At night, you can use this form of therapy for your toning (i.e., Color treatment) because you have a light timer so that the light can be timed at intervals. Each Color affects the body differently, but all are interrelated. Both works together to relax, purify, build and cure. At no point are adverse side effects. It would be easier to unclean a human. But if this person feels awkward.

It is a great idea to wear white cotton underwear because the light can penetrate white material, particularly when it is normal for the skin to breathe.

Before eating, treatments can be taken, but wait two or more hours after a meal. However, yellow can be used at that time if indigestion occurs. Normal light in the room does not influence the Color effect but does not use direct sunlight or other strong lights. It dissipates the Color power. Be warm enough in the room to avoid chilling. As this is the Color effect and not the heat, the lamp can be four to eight feet from the body. It is safest to be lying or sitting down. The pivot on the lamp allows sufficient exposure to various areas.

A light treatment varies from clothes. You wear a good Color for clothes. The light penetrates your clothing and gives you a toning. It's like shining a torch in the hue of your clothes. Some fibres with highly saturated colours, however, resist and diffuse the light.

White cotton is the best fibre since it is pure and does not hinder light. This is regarded as a toning.

You can envision or picture the Color you need or the colours you need. It can be useful to contemplate Color in your mind or concentrate your attention on anything of the Color that you want to work with. A more intellectual type of Color meditation is to put together your ideas for a Color, to let the connections flow or even to write them down.

In bathwater, vegetable food colours can be used to give yourself a luxurious bath. You can Color salt or baking soda to make a salt Color easily scattered. You would like a Color bath in combination with some favourite waterproof stones and maybe some herbs or fragrant oils. Add rose baths and aqua baths if you have a bath (it is on the list of home improvements.)

Violet and dark blue should be used at most for a brief period of 10 to 20 minutes, as both can be depressing if used excessively. Orange is very vigorous and very restful deep clear greens. You should add the petals of the flower to the water. Be careful that the bathwater does not get too hot because it can kill flora like roses.

Art is a valuable and creative way of integrating Color healing into your lives, painting or drawings with the colours that you feel are required. Color can be looked at as a swatch of Color or gemstones or candles, or items of that Color can be seen. One way to add Color is simply to walk in nature and search for flowers. Study the artist's work and discuss the influence that Color choices of artists have on emotions and wellbeing.

Color food can be used. This is considered the diet of the rainbow. You can use warm colours to treat if you are too sad and need to be raised. You may use cool colours to cool down if you are too stimulated and need to calm down. There are a few ways to incorporate Color into your everyday life.

If you are using essential oils in massage or an aromatic bath, you use Color frequencies that contribute to their quality and therapeutic behaviour and vibrations.

How to Raise and Share Your Spiritual Vibrations with Others

The greater an object's vibration, the higher and the greater its effects on the world. Take the guitar case. If the string is gently plucked, it creates a sound, but the sound is also gentle. If you pluck the string hard, it makes a louder sound, and the note made can be heard. The more strings, the more notes are produced. And more echo is heard by the audience.

Spirit beings are like strings of the guitar. The higher they vibrate and the greater their effect on others, spirits or non-spirits.

The question I want to answer now is: How can you increase and share your spiritual vibrations with others?

From body and mind analogies

The professional ballet dancer makes her body vibrate gracefully, often very quickly. A fascinating speaker vibrates her mind, and so shifts her audience's mind. These two examples provide us with a picture of both physical and mental vibrations. The popular thing about both is that there is an operation. The activity is intensified as the vibration increases. And, as it were, the audience catches these waves, one by eyes and one by ears. You believe in these waves. And they're moved into wondering or admiring.

So, the more movement in the sphere of the spirit, the more vibrations it creates, and these vibrations are communicated immediately with others. (Note that I use the personal pronoun "he" to refer to spirit since spirit is a human, not a thing that many assume. "She" can be used as well.)

Therefore, you increase your spiritual practice in order to lift your spiritual vibrations.

Activity Ways of Raising Spiritual

There are many ways to elevate the spiritual vibrations. They are all spiritual practices. Some of these are mentioned by spiritual authors: Meditation is favourite, and there are many strategies to meditate; to sing and hear music; to dance or play the neighbourhood; to laugh and to share jokes with others; to walk in a wood; to forgive our enemies; to do charitable works, etc.

The perfect Way to Raise Spiritual Vibrations

But prayer is the safest way to elevate the spiritual vibrations. It is strange that many spiritual writers do not list this practice to increase spiritual vibration, maybe because our usual definition of prayer is that it is an activity related to the temple/church or a formal assembly.

But the most powerful way to elevate the spiritual vibration is to clearly describe prayer as contact with the Spirit, who is the root of all spirits or with the spirits that originate from him.

You can start with a casual talk with the spirits. Then you will make progress by sharing them more intimately. Finally, you will unite with the Spirit or embrace the Spirit's invitation to unite with him. This is the highest type of action, union with the Spirit, just as the highest form of activity among humans is the combination of men and women, which produces a new human being.

When we are joined to the Supreme Spirit/Energy, we receive his eternal vibration. This is the highest degree of vibration.

Sharing with others of our vibrations

The ballet dancer shares her vibrant body with the spectators—the speaker shares with the listeners her vibrating mind. The audience is pleased and moved to think about the performer's thoughts, admire them or pursue them.

It's the same when we pray. We automatically share the Spirit's vibrations with others. The good that flows to us is shared with others instantly. The one who truly prays or talks with the Spirit or spirits desires the benefit of his neighbours. And they share this fine. Lord

Tennyson, Alfred, put these words in King Arthur's lips, "Prayer works more than the world's dreams of."

<u>Achieving Vibrational Harmony with Your Spiritual Goals</u>

Many times, when we are seeking an enlightened state of mind and an enhanced spiritual consciousness and accepting them, we feel out of sync with our highest selves. This state of mind can be very discouraging when our attention is on good, but our body and mind experience nothing else. Our bodies and minds offer us incredible and clear hints if we do not harmonize with our genuine divine existence. You feel good? Yes, so you are in a neutral or extremely energetic spiritual state of mind. Do you feel bad? Then you stick to something which causes resistance and disharmony with your divine nature.

If you think of the course of your life, all the mistakes you felt and maybe hurt by people or decisions that sounded so wrong, it seems "just" and well justified to make you think even very bad, isn't it? This 'mere' tale, along with some other well-worn ones, that we've made up of doubt, discouragement, shame, unworthiness is what the ego uses to hold us in a narrow mind. These are all the stories the ego has! And ironically, they are all our own mind fabrications and decisions.

Why does the ego that is just another name for our programmed mind want us to be tight and small? The response is straightforward, fear. In the field of our own perceptions and comprehension, our thoughts may be regulated if we ensure that they remain small and powerless. When we suffer, the ego creates into the mind a tale that says that you are a victim of an external source that causes misery. To lose the plot, we just must let it go - it's so easy. But we don't because the story is now a component of our identity, and we fear that losing the story would not make us who we believe we should be.

Our ego allows us to establish all kinds of noble identities, such as:

• When you behave or feel miserable, you are responsible, you triumph over the machine, you defend yourself

• If you are acting or feeling bad - when you show proper remorse, you are sympathetic to your hurt, you lead me to better actions
• If you act or feel doubt, you are realistic, you protect me from danger, and you are modest

Another example is this: "I feel bad because, when my children were growing up, I should have been a better mother/father. That's why my children have so much trouble". Let me ask you, what would you say to a good friend who told you that? You'd say, "Its bunk!" You have done what you can, and your children are now making their own decisions which are the best they can do right now. When we let go of feeling bad about our remorse, disappointment or disappointment, we think we let ourselves go. We will continue to replay and react to this story's bad feelings until it gets so bad it will trigger other problems in our lives and build a situation where we have 'to' abandon the story or listen to our hints (bad feelings) and think about letting the story go now.

Particularly people who have really hurt other people or acted regrettably cannot benefit from holding on to past incidents or the circumstances leading to them. It's never a reforming, deforming habit. Reformation will only come by letting go of this incident and its surrounding emotions and feelings. We tend to want those wrong kinds of people to feel guilty, and we want to make sure that they never do that again, particularly if their actions hurt us.

We believe that the remorse will help them remember their deeds (because it certainly does!) And we will be partly right because their remorse would certainly remind them of their deplorable acts and remind them that the individual who perpetrated them also remains a victim of this situation. This individual will continue to act out of the story until the story about his/her true nature emerges. True correction of any mistake will never come from the very same story.

This is a new way of looking at this bad issue - maybe, when we begin to feel bad and accept a momentary pause in the past with remorse or shame or a terrible glimpse into the uncertain future, we can leap into joy! Why? Why? And from the point of view of fear and doubt, this is a wake-up call! This call says, "You can hear the ego and answer as you always do - or, by acknowledging it and even welcoming it and asking yourself what you must know by experiencing the feeling, are you going to announce your liberation from this bad sensation right now?" This feeling or emotion says, "Something needs to be dealt with here." That's all!

These bad feelings, such as a glass piece in the sole of our foot, where we feel it, maybe very subtle, but it won't harm enough for us to stop doing something and pull any tweezers out of it. We can do it if we resist or discount negative feelings because we don't want to deal with them or because we don't believe that we're safe avoiding them. Resisting negative feelings or analysing them from our experience or future can produce a physical backlash, which could also be considered a "bad" feeling. By the way, it may sound like a big deal to resist a bad feeling or emotion, but it is a sly negotiated with the ego to get a bad feeling now, to allow the bad feeling to be put on for later use whenever the ego wants.

Sticking to bad vibes with resistance or resignation can lead to various consequences in our mind and body that spill our everyday lives and relationships. But there are many steps that we can take to clarify and enlighten our negative vibrations. These trustworthy acts are part of a process that dissolves the lies we have talked about ourselves and allows our higher self to emerge. Some of these processes involve time-consuming activities shared by teachers, sages and mystics of all ages and proved very successful.

Develop an understanding and a sense of openness about your life. This attitude opens you automatically to lift your vibrations of love, harmony, divine energy and happiness. Even a minute glimpse of your true nature opens the portal of pure awareness, which is nothing but divine power. The lack of poor vibration is not a healthy vibration; this is neutral. A positive vibration fills you with divine energy (along with love, joy, harmony, grace) and destroys bad vibrations. At the same time, you can't be happy and sad or peaceful and angry. Take in some or all these ideas and fill yourself with the love and grace in the beginning that the Creator made you.

Practices of life that foster positive vibrations:

Meditation –

Time honoured as one of the most realistic and powerful ways of calming the ego and challenging the tendencies of the ego to discover its limitless god. When we use the process of quiet meditation to allow the feelings and the feeling to arise and move through with inquiry and compassion, the authentic self will be expanded every new discovery. Relax, leave, release. Relax. (Meditation has incredible advantages too in virtually every aspect of your life - oh yes, all these activities, I guess.)

Prayer –

Silent communion with the Divine in any type of prayer meaningful to the person is a powerful way to quickly elevate the divine energy. Feeling the warmth and tranquillity of the moment of soothing grace "still the stormy waters" to allow for more clarification. Asking for guidance and then quietly listening to and welcoming responses, we are in divine flow despite how you feel and KNOW. When you inquire - it's over. Go on. Move on.

Affirmation –

Setting up an ordinary practice of trustworthy claims is an important tool to reflect and drag yourself back to the moment (which is really all there is). Structure your affirmation to be quite credible and desirable for you to be most successful. If you don't really like sports, for example, you wouldn't affirm you're a fantastic athlete, or you wouldn't affirm you are affluent, but continue pinching.

Individual daily practices which improve good vibration:

Modelling –

Creates a model of the individual from a spiritual viewpoint in your mind. Include the intrinsic qualities such as devotion, elegance, grace, compassion and power. Use this model as "other" person in your everyday routines. If you feel bad, stop and think about how this person can cope with this situation.

Reminders and Checkpoints–

Create many checkpoints and reminders during the day to re-establish your vibrational energy and aware spirit bond. Use such items as calendar reminders, device sticky notes and phone alarms. Develop a habit to ask yourself regularly, "Where am I right now?" Be imaginative. Be creative.

Archetypes and Symbols –

An archetype is a model of an individual, personality or action in psychology. An archetype is a symbol for a divine attribute of spirituality. Use archetypes such as angelic, heroic or Greek and Hindu gods to inspire you to accept more vibrantly the divine attributes that you seek. Also, the use of symbols will help you improve your divine qualities by keeping a symbol somewhere that you can constantly see or access. Choose a symbol that is important to you and link it to your desired metaphysical condition or quality. Some examples include a sign of harmony, a lovely drink, and a special kind of nature, like a rock or a shell, or something that you want to reminisce about those spiritual qualities.

I wish you the most powerful blessings as you walk along your path. And note this fact — you have already begun with wholeness. You don't have to find the parts to fill yourself, and you just have to drop the extra luggage you picked up! You'll greatly benefit from finding resources to help your openness to these facts and keep on juicing you with great spiritual energy in your personal and spiritual journey of empowerment.

Spiritual Growth - What Exactly Is It and How Does It Affect You?

For many of these people, life is a sequence of repetitions and events, a challenge every day, regularly, annually and even for life to give meaning to our conditions and situations. Life is also a bitter disappointment for most people, as our solutions are not tangible or understandable. The question starts - How is it possible? Will it ever be found out under this sun?

Fortunately, this isn't about the responses. It's about an entirely different animal - understanding yourself. See, if you understand yourself and know yourself, you can naturally monitor what happens in your immediate environment. And it wanders into some other "larger" part of life. "Larger" in quotes because from the point of view of the fact, NOTHING is greater than you. Well, at least before you can.

It all begins and ends with you - your body, mind, and spirit are all under your influence as a "human being." As you are human, through your everyday emotions, thoughts and acts, you "make" life happen accordingly. Note that no person, religious or political affiliation is listed above!

Defining spirituality.

Now we're in the truly precarious territory, what with the countless personal ideas or dogma on what it is, how to live life, and its connection to you and me in the greatest scheme. But I'm not going to hesitate to begin with, "Life is indeed what you do." I do not believe that "life events" that impact humanity is self-generated, but I would be a fool to not accept that our reactions to these "life events" are also self-engineered. Why else would two people with the exact same occurrence respond differently? This is spirituality now.

Allow me to go deeper. Any case that life gives you isn't and never will be up to you. You have been in this universe, and you are engineered to adjust and prosper as a human being. Of course. But that's all up to your personal preference. Depending on what within you are, you answer to life as you see fit. A fascinating concept of spirituality once came to light, "the phase of realigning your sense of self with something you never thought of." Curtly, spirituality is a self-discovery journey. It is the way to illumination. This journey is BIGGER than us and stretches beyond birth and death. It is as vast as awareness. And it's called "growth" because everything can expand into higher levels with no other end goal but illumination, which is also infinite in nature.

MISCONCEPTIONS OF SPIRITUALITY

Some preconceived notions about spiritual growth you can do to develop spiritually are to let go.

1. Spirituality is pious or religious

Spirituality is NOT faith, knowledge and correct implementation of fundamental and intangible laws. Let me illustrate. "Religion" is said to be derived as a term from the Latin word "Relegate" or "Relegate," which means otherwise depending on the language of the grammatical and who speaks.

The first is simply to "bind/tie/hold back" - to keep one in a certain location and/or prohibit one from going on with something, or to stay within certain limits of behaviour for a particular reason or intent. Used as a case, religion appears to keep you from your spiritual quest.

The second refers to the act of "ride over or re-read literature," which holds one in a repeated state and does not mean improvement but indoctrination. A likely conclusion would be that both meanings speak of being static since there are no better words. Naturally, it might go both ways. One may be positively retained or negatively rooted in the negative state of mind, which inhibits personal self-discovery, spirituality. Religion, whose main aim is to prevent others from being negative, just as it retains others from their internal development and understanding, depending upon the doctrine or discipline that one wishes to permit to live. In any case, it is your responsibility to determine if your faith (if you have one) helps you or prevents you from finding yourself with its 'guidelines.'

The third scenario, which later came from Roman philosophy and anthropology, refers to it as "re-associating" or "re-associating" so that we find ourselves in this loop. These twists - is there a real bond that helps you find yourself? Does a fake religion prevent you from finding who you really are and what your life's goal is? It is also possible to be fully religious but not spiritual. A diligent piece of knowledge can be found here for those who attribute it to Hindu/Christianity/Judaism.

2. Spirituality has a finish/end line:

Spirituality is NOT targeted – you can't be fully spiritual. This is one of the important markers of someone who has no idea that this is a journey. This isn't a destination. And you can't assume that you're satisfied/contented as a human being because you know that you still have space to improve and improve yourself. And if you have this fact in mind, you'll never be "self-just and self-sufficient," not even the most prosperous person in life will dare say this because something "missing" is still there!

Now a little dose of truth. "Illumination" is described as "very qualified to hold and radiate light." It's not a place where you stop evolving and are flawless. Regardless of how far you go, you will hit higher and higher levels. Being informed simply means that you have tools and resources to manage all life energies so that you can make everything around you clear, harmonious and light. Since energy is constantly changing, there is NO LIMIT to growth!

On a second note, there are many directions to enlightenment that take into account that there is ONE destination - find yourself and your place in life and the universe. Choose the course that is happiest for you and aligns with your beliefs. Now you can choose one path at one time and one at another or several paths simultaneously, but you are drawn towards these disciplines. Don't feel like you have to go for something that doesn't appeal to you because other people claim that it is the "right" way to evolve.

3. Spiritual growth needed religious activity:

While you should associate yourself with a constructive faith that provides you with the right resources and tools to explore yourself, these items do not need to be extremely enlightened. You may have learned that enlightenment, the goal of spiritual development, means the recollection of past lives, the ability to meditate for hours, the ability to live in constant happiness, among others.

But many extremely spiritual souls do not have memories of the past, do not spend much of their time meditating, and have no "superhuman" skills. On the contrary, many of them work to raise humanity's condition, raise consciousness, and put more light into their service areas in every possible area. With their lives, they do many practical things and produce many good results. Their work serves as their therapy and offers spiritual development opportunities. They've learned to concentrate up when they're out of action. You do not need superhuman ability to carry out your higher purpose, nor do you.

4. Spiritual growth is Hard:

This is an enormous point of contention. It was said that the process could be very frustrating because, as we said before, it requires that you give away preconceived notions about what it means. Again, "life is what you're doing."

If you come from a moral, cultural or politically correct point of view, then it will certainly be the elephant in your space, so you need to think about yourself from a higher perspective. You can be "layers on layers of old attitudes, behaviours and thinking patterns that are poisonous... and knock down walls." If it, is you, it can be quite an odious task in front of these "demons," which will be painful for you as you start and continue your journey?

Ultimately, however, it is your decision. You can choose to rise with joy instead of fighting! Your mind is a wonder - you obtain what you believe. Do you think growth comes from fighting? If so, you're going to build crises to develop. Do yourself an enormous favour and dissolve any negative images of growth. Give yourself permission to easily find important and valuable things like your spiritual development. It takes much less time and energy to develop by joy than by struggle. Understand, you must NOT work hard day and night, feel tired or overcome unbelievable probabilities and barriers to good accomplishments and spiritual growth.

Some people worry about "too simple" stuff. When the vibration increases, things will be simpler. The real challenge isn't just how challenging things are, but how expansive you can make your vision and how much you can achieve with the saving of joy, energy and creative purpose. If you now have a less joyful situation than you want to be in your life, know that this is teaching you valuable lessons, perhaps how you can go to the depths of your being and learn a new strength and courage. You will learn from these experiences and rejoice in these values. Only reassure yourself that things can't change immediately, but they will change.

You will never be the same when you start your path—search, learning, discovering the greater you are, and uncovering the mysteries of the universe. You will stop for a while or decide to slow down, but you will not want to stand for long after the joy of growth. Indeed, you can never want to quit, as many of you know!

5. Spiritual development is a step-by-step method:

No, it's not got to be. It can be immediate. Think of any quality you like, like inner harmony, a greater concentration or more self-love right now. How long do you believe you can wait to learn these qualities? Tell yourself, "In my life, I accept more of this consistency. I'm now more calm, cantered and caring, "Or whatever suits your choice of quality. You improve your knowledge of these values when you say these AFFIRMATIONS.

Understand that the subconscious mind does not know the difference between real and true. So, use the present tense in your claims - "I am now calm" instead of "I shall be calm" in future so that you can reprogram your subconscious mind to recognize these thoughts as your reality. It creates changes in your life that correspond to this inner reality.

6. Spiritual development is alien to and separated from daily life:

Nothing can go beyond the facts. Spiritual development is YOURSELF's exploration. That is not a better truth. Your daily work is also an integral part of your spiritual development. The payment of your rent, your treatment and self-sufficiency are just as important for your spiritual growth as meditation.

Growth for mankind is due to living life entirely, not to escape life and go to a cave to meditate all day. You are here to learn from every guy, every situation and every challenge. You are here to learn to be completely conscious and present, to bring clarity, harmony and light to everything you do.

Spiritual development is learning from your relationships to your profession to make your life work in every area. As you put your spiritual light into all your work, make all your activities conscious and love, and transform all experiences into an opportunity for development, you are indeed your spiritual self. At first, you will concentrate periodically on it, but as you go on, it will become an increasingly important part of your life.

WHAT IS IN IT FOR YOU?

Better than you ever could imagine!

The spiritual journey can be one of tremendous play and profound inner happiness. Spiritual development provides you with the resources to make your daily life work and to bring more order, harmony, clarity and love into every sector. Your development is the most important thing you can concentrate on if you want a happy, peaceful and loving life.

As you grow up, you can see your life's larger picture. As you connect with the Higher Force, you will acquire more knowledge of the evolution of humanity and its role; you will discover the work of your life and the resources you will need to do it, creating real results in the physical world.

Your life's work is of use to humans, to the kingdoms of plants or of animals or to the earth itself. You're going to love to do that! You can do all the time what you enjoy, and your job can be your play!

Your development will lead greatly to your mastery of life and to joy, passion and life. The more you work on your growth, the easier you can show what you want. Any moment you spend loving others, increasing and expanding your life will create huge benefits. Think of it as a grand gift to yourself, a wonderful treat you deserve and believe, and will, that in this lifetime, you will achieve your illumination.

HOW DO YOU BECOME A TRULY SPIRITUAL AND AVOID POLITICAL, RELIGIOUS AND SOCIAL "CORRECTNESS?"

Within all of us, there is a certain state of spiritual "nothingness" (you could call it a void) in which you can reach beyond your current boundaries, let go of old things and step to your next stage of spiritual growth. There you leave familiar systems, habits, emotions, behaviours and attitudes behind and go further into building new structures that correspond to your higher vibration. You can get insights and do a lot of inner work in this state. The period can be minutes, hours, days or even months. You will be guaranteed to feel this vacuum during your spiritual journey, and your ability to fulfil your duties will help you to grow much quicker and happier.

You are like a bird quitting a familiar jet stream in order to enter a higher airflow by this experience. As the conditions between the two air masses are turbulent and unknown, the bird can temporarily lose flight and fall below the original course. These unpredictable circumstances, however, teach the bird a lot about itself, flying and the conditions which can impact its flight. After all, it stabilizes and flies in the higher flow quickly.

Your vacancy exists in relation to your personality when you let go of an element that no longer suits who you are. While you may not know what to do or how to respond, you may recognize that any gap is marked by heart problems. You will be asking profound questions - "Who am I? Am I lovable? May I get what I'm going to want? What'd I like to do with my life?" It is important to know that only when you stop learning and experience the "non-knowing" in your "natural" way can you communicate with new information. The void offers you various options and new opportunities!

This takes us to the real problem - you must learn how to lift the veils of illusion to be truly spiritual! Lifting the veils of delusion means realizing who you are and what your higher objective is. It learns to see the world in the eyes of your spiritual self, to realize what reality and illusion are. Truth and reality rely on your vibration rate. The stronger your vibration, the more you can enjoy yourself and deal with others. For example, at one level of vibration, vengeance can be a way to deal with the sense of being wrong - vengeance is the reality of that person. On a higher level, the individual can recognize and forgive the wrongdoer of the spiritual law of Cause and Effect. When you raise your spiritual vibration, the reality is spreading, and the veils of deception are gone.

Illusions promise to give you one thing but give you another. Religion (false at that), culture and politics come here. You feel this when you get something that you like and don't give you what you thought you wanted to do. Judgments prevent you from seeing things as they really are, so you really must let your judgments go in order to see past illusions. Learn to analyse, project your thoughts on others, evaluate, or create stories about what is going on.

In fact, when you judge others, you project on them your ideas about truth, and they can't explain it accurately (parents shouting at their children in the shop does not mean that they are bad - they may be exhausted, under pressure or doing what is perfect for their children at that time).

See people without judging who they are, and you can feel better about them. Find and focus on something beautiful about every human. You cannot represent anyone when you judge them by removing yourself from them! Learn to see the wider image of who people are by looking past their roles. It is an illusion to assume that you must be known or highly recognizable as a spiritual leader, whether you have spiritually developed. Fame and richness do not signify one's illumination; both spiritual and non-spiritual people are famous and rich.

Mass consensus, too, that things are somehow illusory. Illusions arise from embracing the opinions and views of others WITHOUT question their validity. If you build new possibilities to make life truer, you must clearly see the world. Only because others do, don't embrace things. Question what you hear and read. Learn to go beyond the normal facts and find your OWN truth. You must learn the truth and come from your integrity, an important part of spiritual development!

What is integrity? It's the fact that you remember! It acts, talks and acts in ways that respect yourself and others. It discusses things before you do them and only does that which you know to be valid - in accordance with your beliefs and values. Don't pretend to be "right," but instead select resources that come your way, not because it seems glamorous but because it contributes to others. It requires bravery, and you may not be confident you'll like what you see before you raise the veils of illusion. However, once you raise it, you will be able to know the truth and understand the spiritual self of yourself and of others and to concentrate on your greater meaning and become your own authority!

Depleted? Tired? Step One to Increase Your Energy and Raise Your Vibration!

Can you cultivate your state of being so that you are protected, calm, caring, energized and inspired no matter what happens? I'm not talking about you experiencing the whole spectrum of human emotions. It's more about how you relate to them. Can you contribute to any moment of inner liberation, inspired energy and high consciousness?

We'll discuss the first move here:

Increase your Energetic Power or Overall Charge

The first step to raise your basic vibration is to increase your total energy. The teaching is basic in Qigong Meditation: gather more energy than you spend. It really is common sense when you look at this. If you use as many resources as you have, you deplete. You've got nothing left. The simple idea of doing one more thing, such as taking 10 minutes to boost your condition, is just too much. You are on the verge of overloading, overwhelming and exhausting yourself.

Therefore, it is important that you control your time and effort if you want to cultivate a high state of being because you have extra energy. You will use this surplus to create new possibilities. Without that surplus of resources, you will still struggle to do it, try to do it all and try to survive. Nothing's going to improve.

So, how do you generate a surplus of energy?

Again, this is truly common sense. It includes stuff that none of us knows. Yet we don't often do them. The demands of the world force us to live, work and care for others with all our resources. They are pushing us toward what we feel is best for us. Ironically, if we do not take time to develop our own resources, we are less efficient and useful for others and the environment.

Given this challenge, energy surpluses can only be accumulated if we commit to taking one or more small measures every day. These small steps accumulate as we consistently gain.

Here are some easy ways to construct your energy load. Maybe you can now pick one or two things that feel like you can do:

1. Go to bed thirty-forty minutes earlier. Every night, even an additional 30 minutes of sleep accumulate over time in a huge energy gain.

2. Wake up ten minutes earlier and focus on praying, affirming, or meditating. How do you feel in the morning when you wake up? No matter how you feel, if you wake up in the first few minutes, you'll feel much better.

What if you think about what you are grateful for in your life when you lay in bed? This puts you in a better mood immediately. What if you spent a couple of minutes praying for thanks?

What if you take a few minutes to relax by taking care of the breathing sensations? What if you found a calm place inside yourself by concentrating your body on silence, quietness and the sense of spaciousness? Each of these clues will remove anxiety and bind you to a deeper, stress-free, worry-free consciousness.

What if you affirm your deeper qualities such as goodwill, joy, compassion and empowerment through clear, optimistic, present-day statements? "I am peaceful. I'm happy. I'm sympathetic to myself and to others. I'm guided and inspired to do what I'm doing here today."

If you do one thing or all of these first things in the morning, you can concentrate and give you a positive starting point for the day and a place to return whenever you need.

3. Set a phone alert to stop what you're doing carefully. Pay close attention at this time to your breathing and check how you feel and how everyone around you feels. You could do so once in the morning, once in the afternoon and once in the evening as a suggestion.

When your memory goes out, you can feel compassionately at this point. Then, take three deliberate breaths and pay attention to your body's sensations. Imagine your whole body fills up as you inhale, and the entire body empties as you exhale. Release your emotions, feelings and pressures consciously as you exhale. Then take care of how others feel about you. Extend humane consciousness to others.

4. Consider all that you eat and drink if it adds energy and promotes health and well-being. Instead of sniffing, pay attention to what you eat. Note how it tastes and how it looks. Notice that you eat and drink food to counteract anything you feel. See if you can do this to the best of your abilities with the mind of a curious observer without judgment.

At least once per day, avoid a normal unhealthy option and instead pick something better. Consider foods and drinks that are fresh, organic, of moderate size and as similar as possible to their natural condition.

5. Consider what you read, watch or engage with as it adds energy to your health and well-being. Pay attention to how you like this material is being consumed. Note the state of mind and emotion in which they place you. Notice whether you use this knowledge for learning and well-being or whether it is designed to counteract something you feel.

Take a few minutes, at least once a day, to read, watch, or engage with content that helps to improve your spiritual and mental health.

6. Stand up once an hour and move your body. Exercise every day for 10 minutes or more. Your body is moving. It's a difference just getting up. Even a 10-minute stroll increases your stamina and health. You pump blood as you run, which carries energy into your cells as oxygen. You boost your digestion and absorb nutrients. And you pass lymph fluid that cleans out your cells' toxins. These are some advantages of practice that increase your level of energy. So, pass yourself in ways you enjoy every day.

As you devote yourself to all of the above, your energy level will rise. Instead of extending yourself, you will be on the road to control and nurture your vital energy. Every day, with small repeated efforts, you can begin to increase your energy charge.

Are you able to free yourself of negative thoughts, emotions and habits?

****

"If You Want to Find the Secrets of The Universe, Think in Terms of Energy, Frequency and Vibration."

~ Nikola Tesla

CHAPTER FOUR

<u>Positive Vibrations and a Simple Technique to Alleviate Childhood Hurts</u>

Positive vibrations are something most people agree on. When we have realized the fact that this is a vibrational world, our time will well be spent in harmony with Source vibrations that are always caring and always constructive.

But what if you were yelled at and treated unpleasantly as a child? Of course, the parent who shouts doesn't have any constructive vibration, and as the parent denigrates the infant, the child is normally locked onto the parent's vibration, and so the action continues.

What is crucial, however, to realize is that the parent often emanates positive vibrations of love and acceptance when throwing out negative vibrations, the Source? That is precisely why the child feels negative emotion, as the parents' disagreement with the vibration of the Universal Source. This distinction is the "negative or sad feeling" he feels. This is what it is, ever! Ever!

I'm sure that you had a situation in which someone was unable to talk for no reason. Many authorities in psychology would claim that you are peeved because your ego is hurt, but the real explanation is that your inner self or the universal self knows your worth deeply as you are, that unchastely doesn't fit the negative emotion triggered by unchastely. If there is a negative vibration, this often means that there is a discrepancy between what the source knows is true of you and what you believe in yourself at that moment.

This problem is an easy way out. You must go from negative vibrations to positive vibrations a little at a time. No matter how much disdain someone had towards you, if you did not reflect on this disapproval, this cannot be attached to you. Simple? Simple? Yes, in theory, but it's not so straightforward in practice sometimes, so what you have to do is take small measures.

Try to transform your mind's whirlwind away from negative thinking. This can also be better by thinking about another thing. Your baby girl with curling fingers, your sleek black cat who shrieks on the sofa like a steam train, your ten-year-old baby girl who embraces you after winning his first football match.

You must consciously direct your attention away from criticism, be it from the past or the present (because they are both equally strong when in your thoughts). The journey is indispensable. It's up to you, too.

<u>Positivity, Your Health Prescription</u>

There are many important lessons in life, but I think the most important is to hold a positive view. One of the Universal Rules, the Rule of Attraction, states that according to our vibration, we draw things to our lives. Our vibration can attract objects that have a similar vibration when we are in a good state of mind. So, because we are happy and up to date, we can attract more things so we can be happy and up to date. But, wonder what we are going to attract when we're grumbling and miserable? Yeah, you have it, more stuff for which you must be grumpy and sad.

And there's something here that might surprise you. Medical experts know that this also applies to our wellbeing. You found this link between the mind and the body. In fact, your thoughts influence your wellbeing. Psychoneuroimmunology is this area of research about how your thinking can have either a negative or a positive effect on your body.

In short, your thoughts produce emotion, and the emotion causes neurochemicals to be released into your body. Positive emotions give you good neurochemicals, while negative emotions can cause pain and damage to you.

That is the reason it is good to have a positive view of life.

Take this into consideration: when you wake up each morning thinking about something marvellous happening in your life today, you always find yourself right. But it's not funny, and we don't often understand it for what it is. We only take it for granted and expect it to be wonderful every day. And while it's wonderful, we still forget that we have been able to pave the way because of our good vibrations.

But the opposite is real, too. When you wake up and groan and whine in the morning, you also have a bad day. These vibrations even came before you to pave the way.

Everything to think about here: if you set the mood as soon as your eyes are open, it can be great each day. Don't wait until your eyes are open, really. When you wake up first, just lie down and imagine your day. Go through it and envision it as an ideal day. Visualize all the way you just want to go. And feel the feeling of how fine you feel. Now that's a strong way to prepare for a great day.

Do whatever it takes to lift and sustain these vibrations. This would not only pave the way for a fantastic day but also pave the way for a healthy new one. Since optimistic emotions are the catalyst that makes those wonderful hormones 'feel good.' Positive emotions often reduce 'stress' hormones.

Now that's a strong prescription!

<u>Vibrational Discord Explained</u>

When you read this book, you know that our emotions are used to provide input and let us know just how near or far we are to who we really are. The more we come closer, the better we feel. The more we go, the worse we feel. Negative feelings are a sign of vibratory discord. But what do I mean by vibrational discord, exactly, and how does it convey examples of how we manifest our reality?

Basically, when you give two different frequencies on the same topic, the vibrational disorder occurs. Your vibration on a topic is at odds with Who you really are (Capital YOU). Your inner being, the pure energy YOU, who is in your heart, always gives you a pure, happy, high vibration of love. This YOU look with this love at every person, being and situation (including yourself). This YOU are completely stable, and you certainly know that you can have whatever you want. Any thinking that is physical to you (little ones) does not fit this high vibration, causes vibrational dispute and, therefore, negative emotions.

Example 1: On the street, you see a bum. He's drunk, and he's raving. You look at him and think about him. "Why should there be so much suffering in the world?" "Why do people like this have drunk? Someone ought to do something!" "I just hope that he doesn't come here and bother me. He could hurt me!" or "I just want something for people like him to do. For him, I feel so sorry. I feel so sorry." In the meantime, YOU - Who you are - look with endless love and compassion to the bull. This YOU never felt sorry for people, because that they are weaker and less strong than you who you know that this isn't real. YOU are never afraid because it knows that you are still protected in the end. Who you never feel powerless because it knows how strong you are? Who you really are, considers the bum to be fine as a whole, pained, and relieved? He's not broken; he's trying to feel much better, the most normal thing in the world. And who you really know that you can only really do anything to support that person from this viewpoint.

Any idea you've got that doesn't align with who you really will feel terrible. Some negative feelings, some far more serious, are subtle. But when you disagree with your pure, optimistic, energy self, you will never experience true joy.

Example 2: You want a new car, really. You're always thinking, "I want a new car," but vibrational, what you're really offering is, "I can't have a new car. New cars are pricey, and I can't afford that. You can't get a new car for me." In the meantime, you understand you can build a new car whenever you want. No sweat. No sweat. This is the sound YOU ARE yielding. It causes vibrational discord when you disagree with YOU. It feels awful that you want something you don't think you can have because you know that you can. Your dissatisfaction with the vibration you put forward triggers the negative vibration that you know.

Now, who you really are isn't concerned about the car. It just wants you to be happy and knows what you want (e.g., if you don't really want a car, you just hope it will make you more desirable to the other sex, and then what you really want is to be loved, you'll know it). But if you concentrate your thoughts on this car, you and you can both give a vibration to this subject and sense it if there is vibrational dissension. Because you always know what you want, it makes perfect sense to sync your vibration with you to show everything that you want. In other words, working purposefully to feel better makes sense.

Your Core Vibration is the sum of all your vibrations. This is the fundamental frequency at which you vibrate (note: you are little). The distance from who you really are to this core vibration creates your basic emotional state. You can feel better on one subject than on another, but if you have a lot of vibrational discontinuity, in general, you will feel much worse than if you have very little discord.

The emotion that you feel about a subject is determined by the distance of your vibration. Who you are? However, the strength of that emotion is determined by the distance of your vibration from the central vibration. Yes, it sounds complicated, let me explain that.

If you get very irritated with your core vibration and think about something that triggers you to get angry, this frustration won't be all that painful to you. Wrath and anger aren't that similar together.

You're probably angry at a lot of stuff, and you have got quite used to it - if you like, desensitized.

But if your core vibration is one of happiness when you hope, and you think of something that makes you angry, that rage will be very painful. Wrath and joy on the emotional level are unbelievably far apart. To make your Kernel Vibration a pleasure, you need very few angry feelings. You're not used to them, and they sound much worse to you than anyone with a lower Kernel Vibration.

This is why you can boost your vibration and overall feel better but feel worse about an issue that didn't concern you so much before you started working consciously with your emotions.

Many individuals, for example, get into this work and have greater difficulties until they start meditating and concentrating on feeling better. They often decide that their work with the Law of Attraction has exacerbated their problems, and they want to leave that course.

However, their issues don't really get bigger. They have just lifted their core vibration, which causes lower frequencies to feel worse than before. You just hear the lower frequencies more. It's like you've got a headache and pounded your thumb. You're hardly troubled by headache because your thumb is very stingy. A doctor repairs and prevents hurting the thumb. But once the pain is gone, you start to see more headache. Sure, you may want to blame the headache doctor. After all, if your thumb hadn't been repaired, you never would have felt your head's pain. Or you might remember that there was always the pain, be glad that your thumb is better and focus on fixing the ache left.

Be cautious, therefore, how you feel, both in general and on any subject. If you feel anything other than content and safe, you don't agree with who you are. Not only does it feel nice to be deserving of a prize, but you can also get so much closer to what you really want.

Become Successful with Positive Vibrations and the Power of Attraction Techniques

Everything that enters your life does this because you draw them to you; that is what we are taught by the law of attraction. Each thinking or feeling leads to vibrations being sent into the universe. These vibrations may be positive or negative. Positive thoughts are positive vibrations, and negative thoughts produce negative vibrations.

For example, your thoughts and vibrations can also be used to draw money into your life. The vibrations you send out influence how good you are and how easily you can attract your desires. You are still changing your thoughts and emotions but knowing them through contacting yourself will allow you to put out vibrations that will bring you good things, like money.

Positive vibration is the key to performance. For example, when you are concerned that you can pay the bills, you are sending out negative vibrations, which can make it more difficult to get what you want from life. The fewer your vibrations are, the harder it is to improve things and think positively. The key to making the law of attraction work for you is to make your thoughts and vibrations optimistic and sustain these thinking patterns.

Here are methods to help you remain optimistic and to send out the sort of vibrations that draw good things into your lives:

1. Every day, you must spend time visualizing the things you want to put into your life. Try to spend 10 to 15 minutes each morning; it's not time or effort, but once you get used to it, the results will surprise you. Over time, the visualization will improve and help you to attract the things you want. The more thought and passion you put into your visualizations, the sooner you can attract your fortune.

2. Contact your feelings. Try to know when you feel a negative emotion; once you can recognize it, you can quickly turn things around and keep your thoughts positive.

3. Music can have a major influence on your vibrations. 3. You may want to start listening to music that makes you feel good and echoes the kind of positive vibrations that you want to send out to attract your stuff.

Your diet also affects your vibrations. For example, fast foods and processed foods appear to encourage adverse vibrations, whereas your positive vibration is increased with a balanced vegetarian diet. You can also adjust your vibrations by drinking water every day. With a deliberate act of intention, you may "charge" your water. You can do this by prayer and meditation - and then you can have the water along with food to help you fill yourself with good ideas and start to send positive vibrations into the world.

How to Stay Positive - With a Negative Vibration Partner or Spouse

People who change into an aware and spiritually driven life frequently find they are yoked to someone who is unwilling to go on the path. The partners are mired in their own negative thoughts and emotions and encounter a wall of resistance to any theme of spiritual illumination, positive vibration or conscious development. Don't despair, and several people have also passed this period and come out with a happier life on the other side. Let's look at what you can do here:

Stay in your optimistic state of vibration. Don't let your spouse or partner drag you out of the universe. If you feel drawn into it, take a walk, play with the children, read a book, have lunch with your best friend, and continue thinking and feeling happy about yourself, your life and your partner's good qualities.

Establish a holy place to meditate in your house, clear your chakras, express gratitude, Consciousness Create an activity that keeps your frequency high, link to the universe. Ask your partner so that you can "recharge" this time. This recharge should help to uphold the negativity.

· Prove how your life changed by being happier, up to date, less depressed, and soon your partner will want to know what has changed you and how he/she can get more!

· Your spouse is bound to have to change by adjusting how you react. If you do something else, that changes the dynamics between you and the family. Your companion will have to adapt or remain up with the new one in certain cases.

· Imagine a harmonious bond. Check out the change in your relationship and see your partner open more conversation, more openness and a readiness to try new ways of thinking. Take what's WRONG down and put what's right and what you want.

· Throw around your "heart net." I think it's a powerful tool for creating love waves that produce vibrational change. See to yourself and you tossing the net of optimistic, loving energy so that it can release your negativity into a net of security and acceptance. This shifts the vibration between you and you're caring and optimistic energy are flooding him or her.

· Spend five minutes every day of the week telling your partner one or two things you love. Instead of grievances, your partner would be happy to hear praise! It may well start changing its perceptions, mood and perspective.

· Focus on the best and the most fulfilling moment you can make and a vision for the future. Release the past. Release the past. Do not reintroduce old habits, preserve them in past conduct by demonstrating how it was before, and make sure that you do not slip back into old negative repetitive relationships yourself. Let us predict that your partner will respond "in the same old way." Open the door for change and opportunity. Make your feelings, ideas, and energy patterns a new pattern of interaction.

· Present constructive alternatives to your partner. When the negative is cantered, gently show what alternative thinking, emotion or perception will foster the wish. Be a trainer, but don't feed these concepts gently.

· Make a Master Manifesto. If you increase your pace, good things will come more and more in your wake. If your spouse or girlfriend is jealous, point out that if he/she follows your direction, he/she will. Then hand a copy of The Art of Conscious Development to your partner!

· Agree that the World offers an opportunity to measure how effectively in the face of an obstacle you can retain your own positive strength!

· Eventually, and this is the most drastic result, you could have to leave the relationship if you have attempted all these over times and are not emotionally sound to you.

When the negative outweighs the positive ones, with little hope of improvement, you have the duty to pursue an alternate lifestyle, alone or with a spiritually minded and more capable companion for your boiling, glad soul. Remember that though children are involved, at least one happy parent is happier with them than two unhappy ones.

For more partnerships, one partner's awakening is often the catalyst for both development and growth. May you be one of them!

<u>Negative Emotions That Can Ruin Your Life</u>

Seven negative emotions exist. Why would you like to learn about it if they are so destructive? You must first know them and how they affect your lives so that you can eradicate them. These are superstition, fear, vengeance, jealousy, covetousness, and rage.

Take a minute and score your attitude to each of these emotions from 1-10 before you read on. A short overview should be included.

1. Fear

Fear is a strong negative state of mind. The two reasons for anxiety are suspicions and worries. How quickly fear can develop in your mind is fascinating. It creates fear. Anxious people usually must see a doctor to prescribe medicine for them. The only way to rid yourself of fear is to face it. Say to yourself, "I'm not going to let fear rule my life." Echo this word again and again. Your conduct is also a big factor. See, attitude is made up of ideas, emotions and behaviour. You can conquer every kind of fear if you have a good mindset.

2. Jealousy

Jealousy has destroyed more than anything else relationships, careers and opportunities. Experts in psychology call envy a fear of missing something that you haven't. People who are jealous aren't happy. Often, we all get jealous. By analysing the origin of the issue, we eradicate this emotion. Ask yourself why you're jealous. I bet you're not going to find a good answer. You're going to see how stupid it is. Substitute order and devotion for this.

3. Hatred

Ignorance is the source of hate. This is one of the most destructive emotions in which a person can participate. How much do you start a phrase with the words I hate? How much do you hear such words used by others? When you get the feeling of hate, you see something awful happening to someone else. When you bring this negative vibration out, you really get something evil. You get back what you put out—the simple law of the rule of attraction. Whenever you want to say that I hate, pause and begin to say that I love you. Repeat this time and again so that you turn your thinking from negative to positive. Love something more, hate something less.

4. Revenge

There is a lovely rule of non-resistance. It's about letting go. Letting go. I believe that we, as humans, must study this rule because retribution is such a stupid concept. Don't even get with anybody. If you give bad things, don't even try to get with them. Only duck and let go of it. Don't play the same game where people want you bad. If you do, that's going to hurt you. When someone does something wrong, take a picture of them with the highest positive. It might sound strange to you, but trust me, it's the best thing you can do.

5. Greed

The cause of covetousness is fear and incomprehension. Greedy people are insecure, so they want to keep it all up for themselves. They're afraid they'll lose it. If you are selfish, you can never get enough in your life. The natural circulation rule is to give it back when you get something. Try not to save it all for yourself. You're going to end up losing it all. You'll be easier to share with them.

6. Superstition

Possibly, your parents and grandparents have inherited the feeling. We have to rid ourselves of all these stupid yet superstition thoughts like, don't let the black cat go before you or do not step under a ladder etc.
If you have these ideas, you have them in many aspects of your life. You are regulated by superstition. Whenever a superstitious idea comes out, tell, "I'll no longer be superstitious. I'm in control of myself." You're going to get rid of it.

7. Anger

Wrath is something we normally suppress before it develops, and we erupt. Literally not. If we suppress rage, it becomes depression. Here's a little workout. If you're angry, write it down and burn it. Don't suppress it. Don't suppress it. Try to always keep a calm mind. Don't let stuff or other people make you upset outside. It's true self-control. Don't let other people rule you. Don't let anyone control you. You must manage yourself.

A lot of harm is done by negative feelings. They cause the body to collapse. They cause illness and drive people away. For you, it's just not healthy. You may wonder: "Andrej, why are you writing about negative emotions for your time?" Since the first step is that we must be conscious of them to remove them. We must evaluate the solutions.

By concentrating, one at a time, we remove them. Let them never return. Let them never return.

******

"Every Single Thought Carries Strong Vibration that leads to physical reality."

- Parth Vyas

CHAPTER FIVE
<u>Your Personal Vibration</u>

Everything in the universe consists of vibrations. Each individual thought you send into the universe constantly resonates, depending on the emotion attached to it at that moment. Just as fire, electricity, magnetism and light are the products of vibration, so do thoughts. You have heard of the great law of attraction before and how you draw yourself to life, individuals, circumstances and situations in proportion to your mind's thoughts. The law of attraction states that all feelings are magnetized and draw like thoughts—the law of attraction. You attract negative entities, events and conditions in your life if your feelings are negative. The same is true if your feelings are optimistic.

Over the years, though, I have encountered several different interpretations, but the underlying message is still the same, you become (attracting) what you think most of the time. It is very simple for many people to reject a rule of this kind as plausible at first only because the vibrations which our thinking emit are not clear to our five senses, but this is not just enough to reject the claims as false. A magnet sends out vibrations and strong enough to draw a piece of steel, but we cannot see, taste, smell or hear the mighty strength.

Whether you believe the Law of Attraction works with the vibration of thought is entirely up to you, but the fact is that the Law of attraction works anyway. If you think of negative thoughts, so it is not difficult to see that you are going to attract negative conditions, situations and face them, only negative people want to be around other negative ones.

Go to Facebook and look at the status messages some people are sending out. All you can find is the same people moaning every day about the same garbage. It's not a coincidence that these people miserably are still there. They think the same thoughts, do the same things and eventually blame everyone else but themselves for everything.

You will also note that their friends are typically the same miserable people that inflate their illusions of oppression with their illusion of truth. Like attracts, the same attracts negative thoughts and emotions. The law of attraction is true, and it works, whether you believe it.

Imagine one day being late for work and you hop into the car and start your journey from home. The thoughts you have at this point are crucial for the rest of the day. If you are disappointed or angry that you got up late and are looking forward to a bad day, you can attract what you expect. Then, if you are stuck in traffic jams, you will become fascinated by emotions that reinforce your depressive state, and so the day will proceed like this.

It's not that traffic jams have been generated by the law of attraction, but as already described, the thoughts which you emotionalize attract similar and similar thoughts. And you are immediately irritated when faced with a traffic jam because your feelings are invariably negative. Your previous thoughts have more of the same, and within the frameworks of negativity, you begin to build your day. The good news is that you can still change your mind. If you start looking at things positively, your good thinking will attract more of the same. You then start creating your day with more chances simply because your mind is in a much more imaginative state.

Those may be what you, me, or most anyone in this situation would worry about, but what is the point? You haven't got a time machine, you can't get to work, but we still seem to be looking at the worst-case scenario of our lives even if the worst-case scenario never occurs nine times out of 10 as it was expected. All you do is create a negative vibration that only has one result. Negative thoughts attract more negative thoughts, which create negative circumstances and situations. Whether you believe it or not, the law of attraction is true.

Confront it, and you can only agree that you are late and know that how you respond to the situation determines how well the rest of your day is. The only reasonable and realistic way to deal with the above scenario Even if you're late and halfway through, the best way to come to grips with the situation is to embrace the facts as they are, don't respond negatively, smile your face and say, hey, maybe this was a warning, maybe I'd be late, maybe I'd have to punch because I know a mile or two down the road, I'll be in a car accident.

That may sound ridiculous now, but it's not a more constructive way to look at the situation if you'd be totally frank with yourself. Wouldn't it be much more useful to look at life from an optimist's eyes if you thought that life would always throw you in a curve and how you respond to unhealthy situations will eventually decide how you view your truth?

If you believe in the law of attraction but live-in compliance with it, you are sure to manifest the abundance, prosperity, joy and optimism that the law itself claims to bestow. You just become what you think most of the time, and you'll see it for yourself.

<u>How to Take Advantage of Your Positive Vibrational Energies</u>

The Universe embraces these vibrations and returns them to you ten times as you manifest a consuming desire. So, what are the high vibrational forces which make your desires come true? Read on to learn.

Love is the highest level of vibratory energy in this world. It remains a mystery how it really works, but it always helps love yourself and others from the heart. But most of the time, it isn't easy because your inner critic is there most of the time to take you down. There are many toxic people around to place you in low spirits. So, amid all the negativities, you need to be strong about your love emotions. You need to be trained to love yourself and the good people all the time in your life. The inner critique and the toxic are tamed with time. That's the fundamental secret.

Love's twin sister is thankfulness since she has the same vibrational power. When you pray, tell thanks for all your blessings to God/Divine Source and Higher Power. Say thank you when anyone does you a favour.

Thank you to anyone who contributes, big or small, to your life. Showing thanks to everyone who needs your vibrational energy naturally.

If you have trouble dealing with love emotion, you should try working with appreciation because it should be easier to manage because it will follow its twin. Try to begin to practice from now on. Good news will certainly follow.

Another way to increase the energy of the vibration is to disperse the laughing gas. Cut laughs and make them laugh around. See your family comedy movies and laugh together. You will all automatically radiate positive energy in a good way.

How do you profit from these vibrational energies? The Universe can only give you something good. Here the twins play, caring, appreciation and laughter. In focusing on every one of them, you put out constructive vibratory energies, and the World embraces them and rewards you in real life for the gift that your fervent goals are manifested. So, dear reader, remember to always work on one of the powers of the vibration, whatever goes to you naturally, and you will be blessed.

<u>Positive Vibration Helps You Hold the Dreams of Your Spirit</u>

When you consider building a better reality for yourself/loved ones, you might concentrate more on the outside world, for example, making money or acquiring better property, or feeling more relaxed starting from the inside world to get your soul or spirit more vibration.

A scientist of the mind has shown me that results from a material-world focus always come with bags or strings attached. But the results from a soulful vibration of emotion will follow this wonderful feeling that you sent out into the world and how it manifests materially will match the feeling – no crashes!

Then it seems easy. Just feel fine during the day, no matter what! You think 'yes, right!' You think.

But what if you could easily come back to a positive feeling when someone or something evoked a negative feeling from you?

Many focusing resources are available to help you reduce tension and retain positive emotions. Simple deep breathing is helpful. If you don't remember, that's exactly what it sounds like. It's not difficult to create time for it either. Here are some ideas about where to fit in your day.

- Every morning you are awake
- preparing your breakfast or brewing your coffee/tea
- When you get to work, just before the day begins
- Before or after lunch or dinner.
- Upon returning home from work
- Prior to bedtime

A few deep breaths taken with the knowledge and repeated many times a day are an important shift in lifestyle for many. For such an easy habit, it is disappointingly productive. Here are symptoms that can be caused by stress to a certain degree:

- Higher stress chemicals that increase our arteries and organs inflammation.
- Muscle tension that reduces movement and increases headaches
- A reduction in immune system effectiveness
- Increased aging and illness
- Energy shortage and self-confidence
- Sleeping issues
- Feelings of panic or distress

You do a very nice thing for yourself with this straightforward everyday routine.

If you want to do something in order to carry on the visions of your spirit, and make meaningful vibrations much of the time, explore a few basic concentrating strategies particularly designed for you. You can offset the consequences and doom-saturated media coverage of a fast-moving lifestyle and gain some control over your precious thinking.

Inner Vibration - Emotions Are the Inner Compass to Wealth

What you concentrate on is expanding. What you do not want to do, feel, or think appears to grow in a direction you do not want.

To explain a little before you get further, you draw more from your thoughts and feelings for a while if you concentrate on something.

This is the pure attraction law at work. What you concentrate on expands when you instil energy into your thoughts and emotions. Energy is all, and all is energy, pure, plain and not so simple.

Let's look at the meanings.

Emotion: a natural instinctive state of mind derived from the circumstances or mood; one or more specific emotions characterizing a state of mind such as joy, rage, love and hatred.

Thought: an idea or opinion produced by thought or unexpectedly appearing in mind; an idea or a mental image imagined or contemplated.

Within: inside or further within; inside; near the centre.

Compass: an instrument with a magnetized pointer showing or indicating a direction or heading.

Prosperity: material success; financial prosperity; prosperity in business and in life.

What you concentrate on bringing to you sooner rather than later. What you want to avoid is to bring you something you don't want by either feeding or to throw energy into or into something you don't want.

Have you ever found that the agony of your punching toe is all you can think about when you stub your toe?

When you centre your thoughts and feelings on something negative like pain, you attract uncomfortable or negative experiences, objects and people.

When you are in a happy or more optimistic mood, you attract more happy and exciting things, circumstances and people.

More to the point, you project negative energy while thinking about negative thoughts such as I hate to be here, hate that work, don't like these people or dissatisfied with your circumstances.

If you think about the many blessings in your life and are grateful, you concentrate on projecting positive energies and gaining more appreciation, circumstances and people.

So, your thoughts and feelings are as plain as they might seem, your inner compass for prosperity.

Negative energy reduces the frequency of wealth. Positive energy increases the frequency of wealth.

If you don't like where you are, adjust what you feel of the kind of ideas you have. Find something for which you would feel better.

Decide to change your thoughts and your thoughts. Choose to feel different, and what you attract changes in your life and experience.

You build your world as you think and feel. This is a method. It can be done, so to speak, overnight, but most of us can't last a long time for an overnight transition or transformation.

What you can do is know what you think and feel and make course corrections along the way before your emotions are even more optimistic.

This is a practice, and the more you practice, the greater your inner vibration and frequency of wealth.

Your ideas and feelings are your inner compass to success. Don't believe me? Don't believe me? See what's happening to you right now.

You generate more of the same in your thoughts and feelings if you're not content with what you have or where you are.

Make a choice to think and feel differently and choose to realize what happens in your life, job and company.

How Whole-Body Vibration Works

The whole-body vibration (WBV), much as exercise, strengthens the body!

While three types of WBV technology exist, they all operate according to the same principle:

If you turn on a WBV rig, the platform moves, but it moves very quickly. This movement is then moved into the body. On the inside, all the tissues are forced to respond to the stimuli.

WBV Works and the Muscles Tones

WBV functions very much like the reflex of the knee jerk. You remember the same reflection that comes from the doctor's office sitting down on the table, and the doctor taps your kneecap. You have no power over the movement of your lower leg.

Your body has no option but to react when muscles are stimulated through a "stretch reflection." WBV technology uses an external trigger - the vibrating base. You then load the muscle group or a muscle according to the vibration path by taking different positions similar to such Yoga positions. Your muscles answer to the vibration as compensation for this by momentarily contracting the reflexes of virtually every muscle fibre.

Remember now, depending on the system and technology, and the platform moves between 1000-3000 times a minute! You can imagine the kind of stimuli this produces so that the muscles tone and consolidate faster than any other exercise.

The vibration of the entire body:
   • Enhances blood flow through the body
   • Enhanced lymph drainage
   • Enhances Endorphin release
   • Reduces the Cortisol stress hormone
   • Trains your sense of balance

You get unbelievable training if you use a WBV tool for training, recovery or therapy. All the workouts are completed up, sitting or lying down. And the pace of platform movement allows you to get the equivalent of 60 minutes of traditional boring exercise at a gym in just 10 minutes with a WBV machine.

The advantages of WBV training are important, as demonstrated by its adoption in major medical, medical and therapeutic facilities throughout the world. There are many health advantages and outcomes that can be easily achieved. Whatever your age, medical, neurological or physical condition, the WBV will increase your overall well-being and quality of life. WBV preparation is not difficult, but it can be hard - you absolutely have the degree of difficulty.

Whole Body Vibration is relatively new on the market. Not everyone is the same, and not all WBV machines are the same. I urge you to learn about technology before investing in WBV equipment to see what happens there. You will be on the road to improved health and wellbeing once you decide to integrate WBV into your lifestyle. WBV is very awesome!

****

"All matter originates and exists only by virtue of a force... We must assume behind this force the existence of a conscious and intelligent Mind. This Mind is the matrix of all matter."

- Max Planck

CHAPTER SIX

<u>Higher Vibrational Living</u>

The layer of your energy body, which imprints your physical body directly, is known as the etheric body. It is the body of creation to what is perceived as the physical appearance. Like the conscious and emotional bodies, the etheric body emits waves of electromagnetic energies. Indeed, the waves emitted by the etheric body are unconsciously influenced by the wave content or frequency of the other layers of your energy body. The aim of the etheric bodies is to evaluate every frequency that you emit from the other levels of your energy self and then form the physical vessel you see.

If you look at your palms, you should be able to see that your contour, the edge of your palm, is a thin contour that appears to match the contour of your hand. The forming activity of the etheric body is this thin area of what appears to be a translucent vapor. Don't worry if you can't see it yet, and you're going to look for it. It will take some time for something new to become a potential life to materialize for you.

So, creation produces, and one of the results is a human being, whether this creation is God for you or no other name. The maker has his own creative expression, and we, as people, are that creative expression. We are gradually learning more scientifically about this as the day goes by. We also experience more spiritually as everyday progresses. In all kinds of developments in the development of mankind, we can only be thankful that this evolution gives us the benefits of this greater knowledge and at any other stage of human life.

If you cannot sustain a high electromagnetic frequency from the etheric body, then it is due to one of the levels of the energy body that does not vibrate at a higher frequency. It is easy to see that you are not physically vibrating at a higher frequency range, and you can experience very recognizable symptoms. If you have physical illness manifested after a period of health, then it was manifested by the connective energy frequencies of the complete energy body, which is you. If you were born with the vibration of disease, it was a chosen and also transcend able course before your Earth journey. All discomfort is caused by the energy vibrations in a frequency range you are experiencing now. The disease has a frequency, and the cells must match that frequency to match that discomfort. Health has a frequency, and the health of your cells must be synchronized.

Unrest after a safe period can again occur from the inside, which means the effects of the energy body through the etheric body to shape the disease. Or illness can develop from the transmission of a misaligned external energy frequency range after a period of health. Knowing this, you will be your guideline to reverse disease development.

Thus, you build yourself, and although you can now start to shape yourself well, certain external conditions can also affect the creation of your physical vessel.

We think you just got to know that you are a physical body with an energetic body of different layers and that you are now grabbing all of this amazing thing (just joking). In fact, this knowledge through the state of consciousness will actively bind you to all levels of your energy body. Yes, you still may have (and for some time) energy barriers, but consciousness empowers you to actively improve just by reading these sentences. Remember, it is your own deliberate decision to make a move.

The external forces on your body are the frequencies of most objects that you get in touch with every day. All in the universe is made up of electromagnetic energy content. The dog, the kid, the refrigerator, the rock, the shoes, the television, the sofa, shades all of the electromagnetic energy, and you are there every day. (Where else would you go?) Some objects have a better energy output or a higher vibration. So how do you know what it is? Because of the slight feeling that meets a specific item position or individual in your physical body. Think of both, the $10,000 check that you have just received in a draw and the electric company's red-letter bill because you don't have the money to pay the bill on the account.

So how did you feel about these two very different things? Yeah, they are both just paper bits, but they wore two very different energy frequencies, regardless of what was written on them. If you either obtain your own energy, body frequency changes to match the specific energy of the purpose when the item is made.

The same effect extends to a position where you may feel higher or lower with respect to a specific place and its reasons. Take the director's office, and it evokes lower frequencies or higher depending on if you are there because of difficulty or because you're there for rewards, but the furniture and position of the office are identical.

People will have the same effect on you if you meet them in a cordial situation or if you meet the same person because of deterioration between you two. Too many of the lower vibrational energy incidences can have an impact on your own energy level. More vibrational energies will affect your own energy body vibration more healthily. Therefore, our aim is to replicate healthy or higher vibrational effects. We can change the energy impact that something has on us by simply thinking about the object, place or individual.

We may also change our body's physical wellbeing by looking at the external environment we experience and adjust slightly. You won't attract the person of your dreams, for example, if you're not the person of your dreams. If we are groaning, moaning individual in life, we attract what and who we are if we stop before we transform those around us into the same sort of person or they are fed up and step away from the world. We continue to reside in attractions like the world and, to attract a happy and prosperous individual, we must send our energy content away from ourselves if we really get what we want.

I never met someone who said that I want to find a partner with low self-esteem. We just don't want to meet someone in this way; we usually follow someone who's happy, smart, fit, nice and ambitious. We have to become that to obtain. To become so, we must line up all of our facets as building blocks for the physical self. You won't show a healthy physical body if you hate to work out. Adjust your mind and watch what happens. You won't be fulfilled if you still weep about the misplaced love affair. Change your mind on this love affair and watch your feelings shift, and the positive vibrations run through your physical body.

Our physical body is the expressive show of our inner selves or the energy body itself, and if we look at how a person smiles or looks over the eyes or steps over the shoulders, we can see the difference between the vibrational levels of their energy body with little eye contact.

A little deliberate self-reflection can be an important guide to why we live our life. It also allows us to transform the changes that we experience into a harmonious, integrated flow of energy in our external and internal reality.

The Vibration - Health Connection

Have you really wondered why we often attract good and other times negative experiences? Ok, scientific researchers and philosophers have an explanation. These shifts are due to our personal vibration or vibrational frequency.

The constant rate of electrical flow observable between two points is vibrational frequency. Quantum science has shown that we are bioelectric entities with electrical currents that pass-through cells, nerves and muscles. Bioelectricity is essentially one of the basic sources of energy in the human body. Different biological processes create bioelectric potential (potential energy) that is used by our cells to control the metabolism of our central nervous systems and brain functions, and to regulate muscle contraction, to name a few. There are three kinds of electrical signals in humans: The first signal comes from the brain, the second signal comes from the heart, and the third signal, of unrecognized origin, is called the electrical surface potential.

Old lessons have shown that we are all able to increase the rates of electric flow in the body and energy systems and that there is a strong connection between increasing our vibration rates and our ability to repel illness, increase vitality and increase consciousness. A high-frequency energy field attracts optimistic, good, happy experiences, while low vibration energy draws experiences that we consider to be negative or unhealthy. There is a strong link between elevated vibration and better health and disease prevention.

Vibration Suppressors

In North American society, stress and toxicity are two key factors that undermine our ability to increase our vibration rates to optimal levels. Different sources of stress (emotional, physical and environmental) and food and environmental contaminants contribute to poor health, unbalanced energy systems, immune system suppression, and personal level vibration suppression.

Vibrational mechanics facilitate stress.

We must apply the rule of vibrational mechanics to overcome the various stresses and restore the prime resonant frequency of our cells, organs and the entire physical body. The first rule notes that a lower frequency of vibration would result in a higher frequency of vibration. For example, when stress or contaminants prevent our energy flow, our vibrational frequency starts to slow down, causing us to lose energy, reducing our ability to access universal life force or prana. As our energy stagnates, our wellbeing falls. Long vibrational conditions lead to a mutation of our cells and a degeneration of the liver, which eventually leads to disease. The lower vibration naturally attempts to echo at higher frequencies by adding a higher vibration level to the lower vibration - and energy balance is restored, and tension released, and wellbeing is enhanced during the resonance.

Vibration Training - Fiction or Fact?

Vibration therapy and targeted vibration training recently took the headlines when Madonna and Kylie Minogue revealed they are dedicated to the system and exercise when they are on a vibrating platform (Power plate, Fit-vibe or Galileo). Vibration equipment manufacturers point out that results can be achieved in much less time than vibration-free systems, such as 10 minutes on a platform is equivalent to 1 hour of jogging. Certainly, this message must really have some foundation.

Research

Data are, however, very incoherent, owing largely to the different methods of vibration application such as vibration platforms, vibrational stumps and targeted vibration equipment. In addition, the procedures followed during vibration workouts such as resting vibration, static vibration training and vibrational dynamics often make it difficult to draw conclusions. Researchers showing that during and after a single set of leg extension vibration exercises (Vibrex, Exoscience Ltd.) at 35 percent of the 1-rpm limit, the subjects reacted in a similar way to the responses that were noted after a single set of leg extensions were performed (Mileva et al., 2006). Training studies have not been completed yet, but these findings indicate that lower training intensity and the inclusion of a vibration stimulus may lead to similar advantages as exercise strength training. Vibration research and implementation are still very early, but an important idea seems to be to reduce the stimulus quantity and increase the stimulus quality. For these reasons, we would suggest always consulting trained practitioners within a training curriculum such as the Human Performance Centre of London South Bank University, particularly at the elite level, who are interested in using vibration for training.

How does it work?

So, what about vibration training that could lead to the above-described benefits? Yeah, perhaps the best way to think about vibration training is to recall when you visited the doctors, and the doctor did a knee tendon tap that causes the lower leg to jump up. This response is known as a stretch reflex. The muscles or tendons are identified by receptors and send an extremely rapid signal to the spinal cord that reacts by causing very strong muscular contraction. If this tendon tap is superimposed on a maximum voluntary contraction, the additional force can be generated. Now imagine this tap 20-30 times a second while exercising. This could contribute to more muscle activity than voluntary contractions alone. We have certainly seen changes in the patterns of muscle recruitment toward greater activation of quick, powerful muscle fibres than in normal vibrational contractions, suggesting the combination of training with vibration could lead to increased exercise stimuli and thus greater performance gains. Indeed, researchers calculated the quantity of work performed by the g-forces concerned and estimated that massive work should be done to match the levels of the g-forces involved (Bosco et al., 2000). The current methods of transmission of vibrations are limited. The most popular vibration training method is that of vibration platforms on which the user exercises. These devices were frequently used in research, but the results obtained are not reliable, although they give potential. Around 30% of people are not able to use this system, as it can cause nausea, and if it is misused, the vibrations can be sent straight to the base of the skull.

Targeted Vibration Training

For these purposes, the concept of targeted vibration is preferred directly to exercise a muscle, which ensures more precise exercise stimulation and eliminates any disagreeable side effects. Targeted vibration training has also been shown to increase power 3x more than traditional strength training (Issurin et al., 1994). In our workstation, we built the targeted vibration system (Vibrex) on small groups of people, and one lady could lift 70Kg one time with Vibrex after 3x weekly training for five weeks. This is a remarkable change. The thesis was discussed at the meeting of the Physiological Society. We also assume that the formation of bones has increased to accommodate this change in strength.

Breathing Vibration Training

A specific vibration system for the respiratory system called breathing has recently been published that induces airflow into and out of the lungs to pulsate to stimulate the breathing muscle stretch reflex. The results look exciting, with a performance gain of 15% after just ten respirations. You breathe currently used by professional cyclists, triathletes, soccer players and rugby players, who claim significant benefits to their activities. More trials are in progress with clinical research to reduce the effects of cardiovascular disorders such as cystic fibrosis, coronary heart disease, asthma and COPD.

To conclude, vibration training offers the chance to boost the return on investment by making a certain effort, but it is still too early to come up with conclusions on how to train with vibration and the type of vibration to use. We strongly advise trained practitioners to include vibration instruction in a full training program. Rehabilitation in clinical groups such as the elderly and osteoporosis undoubtedly have the greatest potential for vibration preparation.

<u>Energy and Vibrational Medicine</u>

Everything that remains is energy itself. A vibrational field refers to the interconnected energy dynamic system. This energy is redirected into different forms by the same mechanism. On an individual, collective level, or as a system or in other systems, a vibrational field may exist. The body system is molecularly organized and is simply a network of energy fields interwoven into one system.

This energy network is organized and fed by small energy systems. These energies coordinate different functions, such as cellular and hormonal functions in the human body. Health and diseases also arise from these direct energy levels. These levels of energy affect growth trends in both negative and positive ways.

This is the point of origin of vibrational medicine. This healing method works on the basis that the vibrational energy which we highly absorb into our bodies mostly affects the vibrational field within our bodies.

Vibrational medicine

The application of various frequencies and sources of energy in the process of healing requires vibrational medicine. It is a promising field in the field of medicine aimed at improving patients' lives. It works by integrating various healing methods that are stronger than even surgery or medications. In vibrational medicine, one of the problems is the use of multiple frequencies and modes of electromagnetic fields.

The other thing about vibrational medicine is that you must work with different energy levels. Vibrational medicine includes various medicinal elements such as spiritual healing, therapeutic touch, homeopathic remediation, color therapy, phototherapy, sound therapy, etc. These aspects of healing are regarded as improving life more than any other form of healing.

The first way of healing that incorporates the elements of spiritual and scientific healing is vibrational therapy. This form of healing is not only the physical body of flesh and blood but the mixture of body, spirit and mind. The cure in vibrational medicine requires the correction of the problems in these three stages.

Vibrational medicine helps the physical body not only to be healed but also to work with the emotional and mental levels. In short, it addresses all facets of the human body by integrating the healing of a human being's body, mind and emotions. It is a promising field that affects every aspect of a human being.

Vibrational medicine modalities

Vibrational medicine is directed at any part of a human being's physical and spiritual body. Briefly, it's a complete method of healing. As a result, vibrational therapy blends various therapeutic techniques that are currently being practiced in America.

Phototherapy

Phototherapy it is well known that the sun is the ultimate light source. Prostate cancer rates are increasing not only in America but around the world. In this respect, vitamin D deficiency is the leading type of nutritional deficiency today.

The sun is the source of vitamin D, and this natural energy has reverted to breast cancer, prostate cancer and clinical depression. It also enhances blood circulation, speeds up wound healing, increases bone density and a vast range of other health benefits.

Phototherapy is used to mitigate the symptoms of certain illnesses by using sunshine. The best time to take advantage of vitamin D energy is in the morning and evening.

Sound therapy

This also requires the use of sound waves to control energy fields in the body and tissues. This is another component of vibrational medicine. It is a promising field in the area of vibrational medicine that changes tissue and energy disturbances. Exposure to music is one aspect of sound therapy.

Color Therapy

It consists of the use of a range of sun wavelengths. This produces emotional, physiological and energetic patient responses.

Homeopathy

This means that the water memory is used to store the healing properties of the material chosen for the treatment in the patient. This approach focuses on a patient's emotional component.

Spiritual healing

It is all about the power of prayer, using it to improve the patient's condition. It focuses on a patient's spiritual side.

Vibrational medicine is tomorrow's medicine. It heals any part of a human being, making the healing process more inclusive. It is also important for diseases like cancer to be targeted.

The Principles of Whole-Body Vibration Equipment - Understand Body Response to A Vibration Platform

This covers one of the most advanced fields for understanding equipment for full-body vibration. It could help you to read it a second time after the first time just to ensure that you don't understand something and miss anything interesting.

In the following clarification, I will be highly technical in order to express the exact scientific principles on which WBV works and how it activates a physiological body response.

Don't hurry through the stuff. Take your time and let yourself absorb it all. Also, don't hesitate to stop looking for a word or read a sentence again. If not all, press immediately. There is plenty of scientific jargon here, and in one bite, it can be a lot to chew.

Let's leap into the WBV Principles without ado:

Research has demonstrated that mechanical vibrations applied on the belly or tendons activate sense receptors, primarily muscle spindles that detect the length.

The muscle spindle's primary ends stimulated by the muscle's vibration help to activate the alpha-motor neurons, which causes reflex muscle contractions. This contributes to a tonic muscle contraction known as Tonic Vibration Reflex or TVR.

The data of Electromyogram (EMG) indicated that TVR is mediated by monosynaptic and polysynaptic pathways in this neuromuscular response resulting in increased motor unit activation.

The effect of vibration is to produce quick rapid changes to the length of the muscle-tendon complex, which aim to dampen the vibratory waves.

Furthermore, whole-body vibration uses movement law to increase functional power. Increased strength, stability and strength in the human body are the products of exercise in which an increased mass is applied or accelerated.

Most exercises and training systems use increased mass to, on the other hand, whole-body vibration devices use an increase in acceleration.

The effects of vibration depend on the muscle's properties. The TVR's response is affected by:

- vibration frequency (number of times the platform cycles in a second, which translates into the number of forced involuntary muscle contractions experienced every second, measured in Hz),
- Whether the muscle is relaxed or contract,
- The extent of muscle pre-contraction,
- Body's location (static) or movement association (dynamic, whether the muscle is shortened or extended), and
- The cumulative effect of all the joint muscles.

Not only neuromuscular spindles but also the skin, joints and secondary nerve endings are used to sense vibration.

This is specifically derived from studies into the effects of vibration transmissions from a vibration platform on the human body. You now have a basic understanding of how the body reacts to vibration stimuli and why the whole-body vibration equipment is so efficient to produce such great results.

How to Increase Your Vibrations?

It is said that very illuminated people have high vibration. People like Jeffrey Dahmer or Charles Manson probably has extremely low vibrations. Your vibrational frequency can be increased simply by doing the following:

Get Grounded

It's crucial that you ground yourself. The most popular way to get ground is to sit in a rear chair with your feet firmly placed on the concrete. Calm your mind, and then imagine the roots from below your knees. Imagine these roots descending to earth's very heart. This exercise will help you to get started.

De-Clutter Your House

If you live in a cluttered, disorganized household, it is difficult to be spiritually safe. Take some time to cast waste, choose papers and do general housekeeping. Think of the waste and storm you threw out. Consider the weight of the trash bags. Realize how much lighter you and the house are making by throwing needless things away.

Meditate

It's so important to keep your mind quiet. Be your meditation innovative. Do what work? Do what work for you? You will meditate 10 minutes just after you wake up in the morning. Or maybe every afternoon you can meditate for half an hour. You can opt to listen to a guided meditation, or you can just relax your mind for a while. Meditation can be performed as you sit in your chair, lie on the sofa or even go for a walk outside.

Cleanse Your Body

Cleansing your body is necessary. Stay away from the doctor's cigarettes, alcohol, fast food, medications, and everything else. It is good to go away from foods, eat a lot of fresh vegetables and drink plenty of water while trying to clean your body actively.

Exercise

Training can be a great way to increase vibration. It can be a healthy way to meditate, as well. You can't quiet your mind when huffing it out on a treadmill. Do something that works best for you. You may want to lift your favourite exercise while you can use the elliptical machine for another user. For certain people, running can be very cathartic.

Listen to Music

Music will soothe your soul unbelievably. Listen to the music that brings you alive. Go with the word "music to my ears." Choose music that makes you happy, makes your body smile and feel great. It's fun to sing, even aloud.

Only reading this book and setting your target helps to improve your vibration. The six tips above are strategies that allow you to increase your vibrations and become more aligned with the universe.

*****

CONCLUSION

What do you mean about your personal energy? We find simple answers from the horses and learn how to change our whole world!

If we constantly communicate by energy and vibration, often without our consciousness, how do we know what we say to others?

It is easy to see while we are with the horses in our experiential learning sessions. The horses respond to our nonverbal energy, and with this live biofeedback, we will learn how to tap our own greater consciousness and extend it with the coherence of mind and heart.

If the horses pick us up, as shown by thought, then what exactly do other people experience in our energy field?

The question leads to the answer, "What powerful vibration do you create in your life?"

Were you aware that thoughts have special vibrations? In other words, what we really think is important.

The molecular structure of water influences human awareness. The effect depends on the vibration of the thinking that you make.

This offers fascinating research about the influence of thinking, words and prayer on the water that produces distinct cell structures in water crystals.

A fascinating knowledge is that the vibration or emotional energy behind any word or idea manifests differently in each of us.

For example, vibrational interpretation is interpreted at several levels depending on the interpreter. For one person, it could simply mean that someone has reached a border, like Karla McLaren in her analysis of messages behind our emotions. For others, however, wrath may generate the energy of anxiety or even projection and fear of confrontation.

Not all of us are the same in our vibrational understanding of emotions under some conditions, but we all know what is good in balance and flow and what is not.

Research has found that the human energy field is primarily influenced by the coherence of mind and heart and that this balance permits one to tap into greater well-being.

This consistency affects our ability to access solutions to problems more easily, but from the position of disharmony and low vibration, you cannot access your intuitive knowledge.
But isn't that where the rest of us are seeking to find solutions? When were the problems steeped in discomfort?

Only imagine that you would harmonize your life more harmoniously through your own internal source of wisdom. What if you have been able to tap into your part that is often associated with personal and joyous expansion?

This spoke about emotion as our focus-based vibration. In combination with momentum, our emotion extends our experience on this level. They referred to a vibrational disk visual.

You can imagine the chakra discs in our bodies spinning. Just like that, imagine a column that is stacked on a vertical plane with several different levels of emotional vibration, each one of which is special to you on the basis that you perceive from the lowest level to the highest levels of emotion. The grid fills up where you concentrate the most.

We all resonate at various vibrational/emotional speeds, and we create momentum all the times... most often in reaction to life rather than deliberately. You are making your own emotional atmosphere, either consciously or unconsciously. We saw a representation of the world of a person in sessions with horses. The cool thing that they teach us is that if we know how we can change that energy in a nanosecond.

The trick is to be conscious of the emotion/vibration/focus you want and then be able to conquer any dissonant emotions until the time is ripe to gain momentum. The more dynamic, the more practical it takes.

When we learn how to use our internal technologies, we learn how to change our lives. By building energy in higher vibrations, we open our minds to consistency, to greater insight and discernment in our personal and professional lives.

Exploring our own energy teaches us how to transform this experience of life within ourselves and how to draw on our own intuitive knowledge. Doing so not only helps to avoid stress patterns in our lives through the synergy of mind and heart, but it also increases mental clarity and wellbeing.

This book aim is to extend the capacity of humans by learning how to live more harmoniously in harmony with our soul-driven life.

*****

Feedback

Happy to have your feedback...☺

Please share your transparent review / feedback / rating is mean a lot for me...

www.parthpvyas.com

Instagram - parthpvyas

Facebook page - parthvyascoach

Twitter - parthpvyas1

Linkedin- parthvyas

For sound healing workshop or any inquiry contact on

Email - connect@parthpvyas.com

Kindle Book / Paperback Books are available on;

https://nexus-stories. com

www.amazon.com

Paperback books are available on;

https://nexus-stories. com

www.amazon.in and www.flipkart.com

https://showroom.dotpe.in/nexusstoriespublication

Jai Hind / Jai Bharat

www.ingramcontent.com/pod-product-compliance
Lightning Source LLC
Chambersburg PA
CBHW061244140726
47998CB00006B/2080